Introduction to Play Therapy

Play therapy is a popular and important intervention for many children with psychological problems and who have suffered traumatic life experiences. Written by Ann Cattanach, a leading expert in the play therapy field, *Introduction to Play Therapy* provides a basic grounding in play therapy intervention, answering questions such as:

- Who can play therapy help?
- What are the best settings for play therapy?
- How should you train in play therapy?

A variety of models of working with play are explored, and an evaluation of the meaning of childhood is discussed in clear language, illustrated with clinical examples.

This book will help adults who communicate with children in any role, be they parents, teachers or therapists.

Ann Cattanach is a freelance Consultant and Therapist in Play Therapy and Dramatherapy, and currently an Honorary Visiting Fellow in the Department of Social Policy and Social Work, University of York.

Introduction to Play Therapy

Ann Cattanach

Brunner-Routledge
Taylor & Francis Group

HOVE AND NEW YORK

First published 2003 by Brunner-Routledge
27 Church Road, Hove, East Sussex, BN3 2FA

Simultaneously published in the USA and Canada
by Brunner-Routledge
29 West 35th Street, New York, NY 10001

Brunner-Routledge is an imprint of the Taylor & Francis Group

Typeset in Times by Mayhew Typesetting, Rhayader, Powys
Printed and bound in Great Britain by MPG Books Ltd, Bodmin, Cornwall
Cover design by Sandra Heath
Cover illustrations by Dave Thompson

British Library Cataloguing in Publication Data
A catalogue record for this book is available from the British Library

Library of Congress Cataloging-in-Publication Data
Cattanach, Ann.
   Introduction to play therapy / Ann Cattanach.
     p.   cm.
Includes bibliographical references and index.
   ISBN 1-58391-247-9 (hc : alk. paper) – ISBN 1-58391-248-7 (pbk. : alk.
paper)
1. Play therapy. I. Title.

   RJ505.P6 C378 2003
   618.92'891653–dc21

                                                        2002014691

ISBN 1-58391-247-9 (hbk)
ISBN 1-58391-248-7 (pbk)

This book is dedicated to Brenda Meldrum in recognition for all her ideas, work and support in the development of play therapy.

Contents

Chapter 1

The meaning of childhood

My Baby
I'm the father of an infant,
Baby mine, baby mine;
He won't let me rest an instant,
　Baby mine, baby mine;
He won't do a thing he's bid,
How I wish that I was rid
Of that awful sassy kid,
　Baby mine, baby mine;
Of that awful sassy kid,
　Baby mine
　Sung by Charlie Bacus c. 1880

Lullaby
Little baby, lay your head
On your little cradle-bed:
Shut your eye-peeps, now the day
And the light are gone away;
All the clothes are tucked in tight;
Little baby dear, good-night.
　　　　　　　　Jane Taylor 1906

Children – our clients

Play therapy is a way of helping troubled children cope with difficult life events. Play is used as the medium of communication because it is the way children make sense of their world. It is the play of the children heard by a sensitive therapist and the relationship of trust and care between the two, which can help children manage their lives. This book describes aspects of play therapy and explores the ways play therapists might work with children.

In the many years I have practised play therapy and taught students about the subject, I have been interested in the narratives adults have about children. Before we can consider helping children it is important to reflect on the thoughts, ideas and feelings about the child and childhood which permeate our society. Many adults talk about children as though they were a different species. Some adults seem quite unconnected to their own childhoods. When they talk about children they seem to be talking about imaginary beings or a different species so perhaps that is a good place to start.

Imaginary beings

In 1967 Jorge Luis Borges published a delightful book called *The Book of Imaginary Beings*. He defined these beings as strange creatures conceived through time and space by the human imagination. He includes in his list such creatures as banshees, brownies, fairies, the eastern dragon, the unicorn and the western dragon. All beings with particular attributes and tasks to perform. Perhaps one of the imaginary beings not listed should come after the Cheshire Cat and before the Chimera. This imaginary being would be The Child. Over the years I have heard many descriptions of this imaginary creature. Perhaps a definition would run as follows:

The Child
An imaginary creature known the world over.
In Western society, first given special status after the Middle Ages.
Often portrayed as a shy, vulnerable, innocent creature but sometimes defined as a wild beast to be tamed.
The creature is often found in domestic settings and can sometimes perform domestic chores rather like the Scottish bodachs who help the household at night when everyone is asleep.
(Watch out for the fairies, they often steal children and take them underground or swap them and leave a changeling. They also steal dogs because humans train them better.)
Some children go to school to learn to be grown-up.
Children live in a special time called childhood, which is supposed to be idyllic.

In time all children transform into adults who are real creatures
and use rational thought.
Adults mostly forget what it is really like to be a child.
Adults make up stories about children because they think children
are different and they want childhood to be magical.
They forget that children are people first and foremost.

What are children for?

'What are children for?' is the heading of an article by Mary
Riddell in the *Observer* (9 September 2001), which describes her
views of the exploitation of children of the Ardoyne in Northern
Ireland who had to walk to their Catholic school through streets
crowded with Protestants shouting and screaming. The children
were clearly terrified. The writer questions why the adults should
use children to support their beliefs in this way and criticises the
use of these iconic images of children as a way for adults to elicit
sympathy for their causes. She then explores the place of children
in our society and comments on the lack of support for the imple-
mentation of a childcare strategy. She states that not only do we
risk losing sight of what children want but also of what childhood
and children themselves are for. She suggests that adults cling to a
Disney vision of childishness not only through nostalgia but also
because they want to annexe it for themselves. What remains is the
sentimental fantasy world adults first contrived for children and
then seek to reclaim for themselves. She suggests that at this time,
adults clinging to the desire to stay forever young, have rarely
resembled children more closely or understood them less well. A
few days after this article appeared, the Human Rights Watch
produced a report called *Easy Targets*, which described the global
scandal of beatings, torture, forced labour, sexual assault and
murder against children by police or other law-enforcement offi-
cials, employers and teachers.

On 11 September 2001 when terrible attacks were made on New
York and Washington, 35,615 children died of malnutrition in the
poor countries of the world. While the world rightly recognised the
horror of the attacks in America, there were no TV programmes,
no minutes of silence or public mourning for the children who had
starved to death. Perhaps we feel helpless, the information is too
overwhelming to contemplate. The sense of who these children are

does not fit into our world or our ideas about childhood. And we cannot connect our childhood to theirs.

Adults working and caring for children

For all of us as professionals working with children or as parents and carers of children it is helpful to think of and evaluate our own ideas and constructions about children. Many prospective students who want to study play therapy do talk in terms of a Disney vision of childhood and themselves as adult rescuers of children. However, this construct changes with learning and experience as students meet and work with children in distress.

Gittins in her book *The Child in Question* (1998) considers 'the child' as a myth, a fiction and an adult construction. We experience representations of childhood from advertisers, television producers and photographers. These images are often used to sell products or elicit donations to charities. Yet we have all been children and memories of our own childhood inform our ideas about who we think we are, who we think we once were, what we believe children are and what therefore we believe the child and childhood should be. So the term 'the child' encompasses a set of complexities and contradictions, which means that there is not such a thing as one child, one childhood.

So the words 'child', 'childhood' carry great complexity and a multiplicity of meanings. There is a cultural diversity in the way we view childhood and yet we have all been children. Our memories of our own childhood are often reconstructed to fit into the narratives of society. I don't really hear my generation talk much about being a small child in the Second World War. How we spent nights under the stairs or in the Anderson shelter listening for the bombs. One kind of bomb was called a breadbasket and I had an image of a wicker box dropping from the skies. I do remember my Mickey Mouse gas mask. How I loathed that mouse face quite dark and frightening, and the smell of rubber when it was fitted over the face. Did the adults really think that Mickey Mouse would be less frightening or make it better? I liked the ordinary mask much more: it was less frightening, but I recognised I had to appease the adults and reassure them so I said that Mickey Mouse was fun.

Some years ago I ran a reminiscence group in an old people's home and reminiscence about childhood was a popular subject.

Initially the descriptions of childhood seemed to be idyllic and romantic until one day one old lady asked the group to stop talking. She wanted to say that her childhood had not been idyllic at all. She had been abused and battered by her father. She described the fear and the misery. She looked at the group with a wry smile. 'There' she said 'I have never spoken about this before.' There was a powerful silence and we were all aware that having let go of her secret sadness perhaps at last she could rest with dignity and honesty. She died three days later. We hold onto our secrets if we feel they conflict with the received view.

Many adults use children to satisfy their own fantasies but do not acknowledge this, so they are unable to negotiate with children. Just last week I was talking to two children who were describing their attic to me. It has a rail track and trains and their daddy spends such a lot of time there. Daddy's track and daddy's train although ostensibly bought for the children. They didn't want the train but wanted to appease their parents. They would have liked a playroom with toys and beanbags to throw and lie on, not trains, which they are not allowed to touch let alone use for play. So the children play outside on their bikes or with the stones in the road while daddy sits in isolated splendour with the trains and the track. The children are tolerant of his needs more than he is tolerant of theirs. When he is angry he says they are ungrateful. 'Look what I've made for you,' he says.

Adults often communicate with children as though they are a different species and children often recognise this and respond by playing at being children to appease the adults. The French philosopher Baudrillard (1993) was aware of this when he described the relationship between adults and children as subtlety. He writes that the strategies adopted to make this relationship are twofold. The adults make children believe they, the adults, are adults, while children for their part let adults believe that they, the children, are children. Of the two strategies, the second is the subtler, for while adults believe they are adults, children do not believe that they are children. They *are* children but they do not believe it. So daddy plays with his train believing he is an adult and has created the train for these children and the children play at being children to appease their father so he can use them as an excuse for his desire to play trains.

Baudrillard states that childhood haunts the adult universe as a subtle and deadly presence and it is in this sense that the child is other to the adult: the child is the adult's destiny, the adult is his most subtly distilled form.

Definitions of childhood and children

To return to Gittins' definitions, the child is a myth, a fiction, an adult construction. So is childhood. Both have become symbolically central to our culture and psychologically crucial to our own sense of self.

She states that the child denotes an individual, embodied being, that is, in one way or another, not adult. The child is a transitory being, changing, growing, developing and this leads to confusion when defining the child. What fits a 3-year-old is different to a 17-year-old. While the child is defined as an embodied being the term also connotes dependency, powerlessness and whatever a culture uses to define the non-adult. In some cultures for example, women, slaves, the insane have been defined as not fully mature and so like children. However, once we begin to generalise about the group, individual differences can be lost.

One of the delights of tales and stories is the way the child is described as an individual coping with the strange complexities of the adult world. Read *Master of All Masters* and ponder who is the child.

> *Master of All Masters*
> A girl once went to the fair, to hire herself for a servant. At last a funny-looking old gentleman engaged her. And took her home to his house.
> When she got there he told her he had something to teach her for that in his house he had his own name for things. He said to her 'What will you call me?'
> 'Master or mister or whatever you please, sir' she said.
> He said: 'You must call me master of all masters. And what would you call this?' pointing to his bed.
> 'Bed or couch or whatever you please sir.'
> 'No that's my barnacle. And what do you call these?' said he pointing to his pantaloons.
> 'Breeches or trousers or whatever you please sir.'
> 'You must call them squibs and crackers. And what would you call her?' pointing to the cat.
> 'Cat or kitty or whatever you please sir.'

'You must call her white-faced simminy and this,' now showing the fire 'what would you call this?'
'Fire or flame or whatever you please sir.'
'You must call it hot cockalorum, and what is this?' he went on pointing to the water.
'Water or wet or whatever you please sir.'
'No pondalorum is its name. And what do you call all this?' he said pointing to the house.
'House or cottage or whatever you please sir.'
'You must call it high topper mountain.'
That very night the servant woke her master up in a fright and said
'Master of all masters get out of your barnacle and put on your squibs and crackers.
For white-faced simminy has got a spark of hot cockalorum on it's tail and unless you get some pondalorum high topper mountain will be all on hot cockalorum.
That's all.'

While 'the child' carries many contradictory meanings, childhood is by definition a social and cultural concept, and becomes an idea as well as a category but never refers to an individual embodied child. So childhood indicates an ill-defined period of time as variously defined by adults. Gittins suggests that a culture might have a word for 'child' without necessarily having a concept of child*hood.*

Childhood suggests a different, separate, other group. Baudrillard suggests that adults use this 'otherness' and that we live not through our own energy but through the energy we subtly spirit away from the otherness of children.

In *Managing Monsters* (1994), Warner describes childhood as special and magical, precious and dangerous at once. In our society, this special sphere of childhood has grown as a social concept, as a market possibility, as an area of research, as a problem. She considers that contemporary child mythology enshrines children to meet adult desires and dreams and we call children 'little devils', 'little monsters', 'little beasts' with the full ambiguous force of the terms, all the complications of love and longing, repulsion and fear.

Perhaps we need to explore the history of childhood to place present ideas in context with the past.

Historical definitions

We often forget that childhood has a history. The first major works in the history of childhood were those of Philippe Aries, *Centuries of Childhood* (1960 (1986)) and Lloyd De Mause, *The History of Childhood* (1976). These were called 'grand stage theories'.

Philippe Aries

In *Centuries of Childhood*, Aries presents the idea that childhood is socially and historically constructed. He suggests that representations of children have changed over time so children have not always existed in the way we perceive them in the twenty-first century.

He considered that ancient societies may well have understood the differences between children and adults and understood child development and its necessity but these concepts of children were not present in the Middle Ages. It is from this medieval absence of the concept of childhood that our current view of the child has evolved.

Aries draws his material from art, iconography, religion and education. The sources are French but his thesis is generalised in relation to the rest of the western world.

He suggests that up to and including the Middle Ages there was no collective perception of children as essentially different from anyone else. At that time status was not determined by age or physical maturity. As soon as a child could live without his mother's infant nurture he belonged to adult society. This absence of the definition of what belonged to childhood extended to games, crafts and arms. Aries developed these ideas from his observation of paintings and iconography of the period. He recorded the fact that children were almost totally absent from medieval paintings and where they were presented were shown as miniature adults.

He states that medieval art until about the twelfth century did not know childhood or did not attempt to portray it. He considered it hard to believe that this neglect was due to incompetence or incapacity but it seems more probable that there was no place for childhood in the medieval world. The history of representations of childhood is also gendered because when children were first represented in family portraiture it was boys who were shown as a special social category, and not just boys but middle-class boys, who went to school as far back as the late sixteenth century.

Aries believes that the first recognition and interest in childhood emerged in the sixteenth and seventeenth centuries when childhood was seen as a time of innocence and sweetness. He defined this time as the coddling period. This is the first time that in upper class portraits children wore special costumes to mark them out from adults. The change of clothing marks a shift in the general attitude towards children who became a source of amusement and relaxation for adults. Children were pampered; adults played with them and took delight in their physical presence. However, they were still part of the adults' world and not separated out as a special group. Much of course depended on the economic resources of families and for most people children remained a potential source of economic contribution to the family.

There was a reaction to 'coddling' in the seventeenth century largely led by churchmen and pedagogues which Aries defined as the moralistic period. Children were perceived as fragile creatures that needed to be both safeguarded and reformed. Children must be trained and disciplined as a preparation for adult life. These ideas laid the groundwork for the development of child psychology and greatly influenced ideas about childhood and child rearing up to contemporary times.

These two concepts of childhood, coddling and disciplining, passed into family life and in the eighteenth century were added concern about hygiene and physical health.

So a coddling rhyme:

Lullaby
Alie balie alie balie bee
Sittin' on your mammie's knee:
Greetin' for a wee bawbee
To buy some sugar candy.

A rhyme for discipline:

Miss Sophia
Miss Sophy, one fine sunny day,
Left her work and ran away;
When soon she reach'd the garden gate,
Which finding locked, she would not wait,
But tried to climb and scramble o'er
A gate as high as any door.

But little girls should never climb,
And Sophy won't another time;
For when, upon the highest rail,
She lost her hold, and sad to tell,
Was hurt and bruised – for down she fell.

And health:

Caroline Pink
Caroline Pink, she fell down the sink,
She caught the Scarlet fever,
Her husband had to leave her.
She called the doctor Blue,
And he caught it too –
Caroline Pink from China Town.

The philosophy of the eighteenth-century Enlightenment developed ideas about the study of childhood, the education of the child, and the process of growing up. The child becomes a new category of being, fragile and vulnerable yet at the same time ripe for correction and training.

Aries considered that the family and school together removed the child from adult society. The school shut the child in a disciplinary system and the solicitude of family, church, administrators and moralists deprived the child of the freedom previously enjoyed among adults. The modern family satisfied a desire for privacy and also a craving for identity. Aries does not see this as positive development and bemoans the removal of the child from adult society.

Lloyd De Mause

Lloyd De Mause presents what he called a psychogenic theory of history in which the evolution of parent–child relations constitutes an independent source of historical change. He considers the history of childhood to be a series of closer approaches between adults and child, with each closing of psychic distance producing fresh anxiety. The reduction of this adult anxiety is the main source of the child-rearing practices of each age.

De Mause considers the history of childhood is the history of child abuse.

Consider the parenting of Punch and Judy, a popular street entertainment for over three hundred years.

Punch and Judy
Judy re-enters after Punch has thrown the baby among the spectators:

Judy: Where is the child?
Punch: Gone – gone to sleep.
Judy: What have you done with the child, I say?
Punch: Gone to sleep, I say.
Judy: What have you done with it?
Punch: What have I done with it?
Judy: Ay: done with it! I heard it crying just now. Where is it?
Punch: How should I know?
Judy: I heard you make the pretty darling cry.
Punch: I dropped it out of the window.
Judy: Oh you cruel horrible wretch, to drop the pretty baby out of the window. Oh! You barbarous man.
Punch: You shall have another one soon, Judy, my dear. More where that came from.

The baby is expendable, an it, an object, not a he or a she, and easily replaced. Don't get too attached, lots of babies die anyway. And for the children watching the performance, Mr Punch articulates their greatest fear, that of being hurt and abandoned by your parents.

De Mause describes six child-rearing modes, which he claims operate in historical progression. He uses aspects of Freudian theory to explain these modes and describes three reactions of adults when they are face-to-face with a child who needs something. The adult can use the child as a vehicle for projection of his own unconscious, he can use the child as a substitute for an adult figure important in his own childhood or he can empathise with the child's needs and act to satisfy them.

These psychological processes used by adults when dealing with children are placed in a linear historical context by de Mause. The six child-rearing modes of infanticidal, abandoning, ambivalent, intrusive, socializing and helping are presented as a historical-evolutionary scheme driven by increasingly closer approaches between adults and children. He considers that more and more adults see children as separate individuals, rather than split-off aspects of their own sexual and aggressive unconscious material. De Mause also recognises that this linear description does not include all child rearing in families in the twentieth century, but there is more awareness of the needs of children.

Critique of grand stage theorists

A number of historians and modernisation theorists have criticised the grand stage theories of Aries and De Mause. Modernisation theorists would question the application of Freudian theory to earlier historical periods or assume that such theories are universal. The theories do not allow for cultural variation or variations between social classes and groups. However it is important that there is a history, which has focused on the emotional value of children to parents.

In *Forgotten Children* (1983), Pollock claims that parents have always valued their children. She concentrates her sources on adults' diaries and autobiographies to consider parent-child relationships and found that in the sixteenth century, concepts of childhood did exist in that children were perceived as different from adults and required protection. Pollock gives examples of parents enjoying their children's company from the sixteenth century onwards and from her sources children were not subjected to brutality and their relationship with their parents was more informal than supposed. Pollock's material is taken from 500 British and American diaries, autobiographies and connected sources. She found that children and parents were close to each other and influenced by each other. Pollock considers that aspects of parental care such as protection, love and socialisation are essential for survival but she does not explore what these values might have meant to, for example, fourteenth-century parents. The selection of her material has also been questioned; diaries and autobiographies coming from the literate upper classes who might also have omitted aspects of their lives which might present them in a bad light.

A new history of childhood

Until the new history of childhood all the research has focused on what adults think of childhood. The new history hopes to explore the history of childhood from the perspective of the children, their relationships with each other and their interactions with adults. An example of this approach is the work of Hanawalt, *Growing up in Mediaeval London* (1993). This work uses evidence from court records, coroners' rolls, literary sources and books of advice to describe the lives of London children in the fourteenth and fifteenth centuries.

Hanawalt considers that the Middle Ages did recognise stages of life that corresponded to childhood and adolescence. These two life stages appeared in learned texts and in literary works and the folk terminology of the period. Londoners described youth as 'wild and wanton' and adulthood as 'sad and wild'.

She challenges ideas that children were harshly treated and produces evidence of children playing; such games as ball and tag, racing and playing with hoops. Children also participated in local festivals and celebrations. She states that children were seen as different from adults and requiring different treatment. There were the usual exhortations from the sad and wise adults. In *Lessons of Wisdom for All Manner of Children*, a medieval book of manners, Symon wrote:

> Child, climb not over house nor wall,
> For no fruit, birds or ball.
> Child, over men's houses no stones fling,
> Nor at glass windows no stones sling.
> And child, when thou goest to play,
> Look thou come home by light of day.
> (Symon, in Hanawalt, 1993, pp. 123–125)

Jamieson and Toynbee (1992) explored growing up from 1900 to 1930 in their book *Country Bairns*. They describe the lives of children in crofting communities, farm servants' children and farmers' children in Scottish society through interviews with elderly people who explored aspects of their lives as children. The authors state that life is described from the perspective of children and young people, although it is as remembered rather than a living childhood and youth; this might suggest that the book is not about the lives of children but the childhood memories of adults.

However, it is fascinating to read of the economic and cultural influences on parenting in these particular communities. The authors note that the children had no childhood in the sense of a particular special time free from the responsibilities of adulthood, deserving tolerance and indulgence from adults and allowing time to develop one's potential as an individual. None of the children had toys and there were few entertainments designed specifically for children. The children played while they worked, when they were coming home from school, and the children who lived on farms played in the fields around the farm.

There was a degree of deference between fathers and children across all classes and occupational groups. Many mothers were also distant figures because of their domestic work but even in the better-off households, mothers did not necessarily consider spending time with their children as a priority. At this time adults rarely regarded themselves as being at the service of their children. The children did not have easy access to their parents in the way of talking about their fears and problems.

So one of the farm servants stated:

> *Did you have time to play when you were at school?*
> Oh yes. But there was only ourselves and . . . the other families moved occasionally – sometimes there were other children, sometimes mebbe no. The nearest neighbours was about a mile. They would turn up on a Saturday.
> *Did you ever play with your parents?*
> They would never have time to play. . .
> *Did you tell stories to while away the time?*
> I suppose there would be. My father used to read sometimes at night. But the main thing was getting the old rug finished.

The authors conclude that there is little evidence to suggest that parents showed any great degree of sensitivity to the needs of children and all these children were seen and treated more like small adults than children are today. Yet at the same time some aspects of adult life were absolutely closed to them, for example, the children did not discuss sexual matters with their parents.

Adult memories of childhoods of long ago make fascinating reading. In *The Scotswoman At Home and Abroad* (McMillan 2000), a book of non-fictional writing from 1700–1900, Lady Anne Lindsay Barnard (1750–1825) describes her childhood memories. She was the eldest of eight boys and three girls. Her mother married at 22 when her father was 60.

> To my mother Lord Balcarres gave up the entire management of the family and the children; he knew her prudence and

rarely interfered in her jurisdiction, except when he found little misdemeanours punished as crimes, and then I have heard him say, 'Odsfish, Madam! you will break the spirits of my young troops, – I will not have it so!' – But while the tearing of clothes or fracturing of tea-cups might be too rigorously chastised, or while the needless privations might be imposed on us to fit us 'for the hardships of life', let us not forget that from Lady Balcarres' conversation and practice we learnt those general rules of equity and honour, of independence of mind and truth, which have through life, I am convinced governed the mind of many a brother.

Had she accompanied this sometimes with a little of a mother's fondness, what a foundation of tenderness as well as veneration would have been laid in our hearts! But unfortunately for the contents of our nursery, it was not the system of that century [1700] to treat children with gentleness; everything was done by authority and by correction.

(McMillan, 2000, p. 50)

Lady Anne goes on to describe the day the children ran away from home to another family at the suggestion of her sister Margaret who thought they would do much better with that family than 'the 'horrous life we live at home'. The escape was planned in the privy where the children hid to eat items stolen from the kitchen and garden.

The proposal was agreed to with acclamations of joy, and we instantly set out on the journey, intending by forced marches to reach the neighbour's house that night, as it was but three miles distant and by the side of the sea; but as we could not think of leaving little James behind, who had not yet got into breeches, it considerably retarded us, as we had to carry him by turns. Our flight was discovered by Auld Robin Grey, the shepherd – 'All the young gentlemen and young ladies and all the dogs are run away, my lady!' – a messenger being dispatched, not to negotiate but to bring us back nolens volens, the six criminals were carried before the Countess, who declared that on this occasion whipping was too good for us, and that we should each have a dose of tincture of rhubarb to teach us to stay at home – a punishment classically just in its last degrees, as the eldest, consequently the most guilty, had the last and most offensive glass of the bottle.

From Lives of the Lindsays. Vols. II and III
(McMillan, 2000, p. 50)

Margaret described their home as a place with 'hard laws and little play'. Robert, who was often chastised and shut in a closet, cared for his mother in her old age. Lady Anne remarked about Robert that 'thoroughly good minds pardon severity arising from right meanings'. Did she feel guilty about her treatment of Robert? Perhaps his brothers and sisters were his consolation and support in childhood so he was able to forgive the harsh treatment he received from his mother.

Social theories of childhood

According to Jenks (1996), the idea of childhood is not a natural but a social construct and as such its status is constituted in particularly socially located forms of discourse. So if the child is being thought about in the common-sense world or the disciplined world of specialisms the meaningfulness of the child as a social being derives from its place and purpose in theory. This means that the child is always presented to serve the purposes of supporting and perpetuating the versions of humankind, action, order, language and rationality within particular theories.

Key discourses about childhood in the twentieth century have emerged from the theories of developmental psychologists, in particular Swiss psychologist Jean Piaget, Russian psychologist Lev Vygotsky and English child psychoanalyst, John Bowlby.

While Piaget tried to show how logical thinking in children develops out of its biological roots, Vygotsky was interested in the special role language plays in human society and social thought; Bowlby was concerned with the role of social relationships between parent and child in the formation of personality and well-being.

In Piaget's account of child development, human knowledge can be considered as if it were a biological 'organ' of the mind. Acquiring knowledge can be considered as an evolutionary process in the sense that knowledge is adaptive. It is an evolutionary process in that later stages succeed earlier stages because they are more adaptive, that is more adequate to the demands of reality. So child development has a particular structure, which consists of a series of predetermined stages leading to the eventual achievement of logical competence. Piaget describes four main stages for intellectual development. These are the sensori-motor stage from birth to 2, which ends with the acquisition of thought and language; the pre-operational stage from 2 to about 7 when the child has yet to acquire fully logical thinking; the concrete operational stage from 7 to about 12 when the child can make deductions about the concrete properties of things; and finally, the formal operational stage, a form of thought acquired by adolescents in western society.

These stages are chronologically ordered but also arranged in a hierarchy of status from the low status of sensory thought to the high status of 'operative' intelligence. Piaget regarded children's play as a trivial activity distracting from the task of childhood, which is to develop adult cognitive competence.

Piaget considers that the child is appropriately adapted to the environment when a balance has been achieved between accommo-dation and assimilation. Assimilation is described as the absorption and integration of new object experiences into existing schemata, whereas accommodation requires the modification of existing schemata or the construction of new ones to incorporate new and discordant object experiences.

Piaget's theories have greatly influenced the narrative of child-hood and the way children are taught in schools. His emphasis on the high status of rational thought has led to play being considered as a marginal activity in childhood rather than the way children learn about their social world.

Vygotsky was concerned to show how culture influences the course of development. He uses culture to describe the customs of a particular people at a particular time and their collective intellec-tual, material, scientific and artistic achievements over historical time. He considers that speech pre-eminently has the role for carrying culture. Language both stores and carries the historical stock of social experiences and is the tool of thought. Vygotsky placed a much greater emphasis than Piaget on the formative role of culture in development. He saw a close link between the acqui-sition of language and the development of thinking and emphasised the importance of social interaction in development. He developed a theory of the zone of proximal development (ZPD), which can be defined as the difference between what a child can achieve unaided in solving a problem and what can be achieved with the help of adults or with the peer group. Vygotsky related play to the ZPD as a way in which the child tries out adults' roles such as mother, father, teacher, and also uses toys and other cultural artefacts in play.

Bowlby's theory is concerned with the emotional development of the child. His attachment theory states that the primary carer, usually the mother, provides a secure base from which the developing infant can explore the world and periodically return to safety. The evolutionary function of such attachments is thought to protect the child from predators, provide for basic survival in the short term, and lead to the reproductive success of the species. A secure attachment is thought to lead the child to a range of psychologically healthy developmental pathways, which will be replicated in attachments across the life cycle.

Sociologists have examined the dominant narratives about the child current in the twentieth century. Hendrick (1990) describes a variety of models of the child, which emerged from 1880 on. He describes aspects of childhood which were emphasised at particular times. The constructions which emerged are, in chronological order, the romantic child, the evangelical child, the factory child, the delinquent child, the schooled child, the psycho-medical child and the welfare child. Then two further reconstructions: the psychological child, the family child, and the public (child in a care system) child.

James and Prout (1990) proposed a new paradigm for the sociology of childhood:

1. Childhood is understood as a social construction. As such it provides an interpretive frame for contextualising the early years of human life. Childhood, as distinct from biological immaturity, is neither a natural nor universal feature of human groups but appears as a specific structural and cultural component of many societies.
2. Childhood is a variable of social analysis. It can never be entirely divorced from other variables such as class, gender and ethnicity. Comparative and cross-cultural analysis reveals a variety of childhoods rather than a single and universal phenomenon.
3. Children's social relationships and cultures are worthy of study in their own right, independent of the perspective and concerns of adults.
4. Children are and must be seen as active in the construction and determination of their own social lives, the lives of those

around them and of the societies in which they live. Children are not just the passive subjects of social structures and processes.

5. Ethnography is a particularly useful methodology for the study of childhood. It allows children a more direct voice and participation in the production of sociological data than is usually possible through experimental or survey styles of research.

6. Childhood is a phenomenon in relation to which the double hermeneutic of the social sciences is acutely present. That is to say, to proclaim a new paradigm of childhood sociology is also to engage in and respond to the process of reconstructing childhood in society.

Conclusion

The way we view children and childhood is complex. Jenks (1996) states that in one sense we get the children we deserve and that our perspectives on normality in childhood reflect the changes in the organisation of our social structures.

Warner (1994) states that contemporary child mythology enshrines children to meet adult desires and dreams. As a therapist working with children I have heard a variety of narratives about childhood problems and some of these fit into child as monster to be reformed and child as innocent to be controlled. Perhaps we need to listen to the children we know and help them represent their own views of their circumstances. This is a complex endeavour because what children want may not be possible but it is important to listen and respect their voices.

Narratives on childhood through the ages

The Two Pickpockets (English Folk Tale)
Once there was a provincial pickpocket who was very successful at his work and he thought he would go up to London to see what he could do there. So he went up to London and he was very successful there.

One day as he was busy in Oxford Street he discovered that his own wallet had been taken. He looked round and saw a very smart girl walking away. He was sure she was the one who had picked his pocket, so he followed her and got his wallet back from her. He was very impressed by her cleverness in taking his wallet. He suggested that they should go into partnership together. And so they did and they were very successful as a pair.

After a time, the pickpocket thought 'We're the best pickpockets in London. If we married we could breed up a race of the best pickpockets in the world.' So he asked the girl, she was quite agreeable and they were married. In time a beautiful baby boy was born to them. But the poor baby's right arm was bent to his chest and the little fist tightly clenched. And nothing they could do would straighten it.

The poor parents were very sad. 'He will never make a pickpocket with a paralysed right arm.' They took him at once to the doctor but the doctor said he was much too young to be helped and they must wait. But they didn't want to wait. They took him to one doctor after another and at last, because they were very rich by this time, to the best child specialist they could hear of.

This specialist took out his gold watch and felt the pulse on the paralysed arm. 'The flow of blood seems normal,' he said. 'What a clever little baby he is for his age, he's focusing his eyes on my watch.' He took the chain out of his waistcoat and swung the watch to and fro, and the baby's eyes followed it. Then the little bent arm straightened out towards the watch, the little clenched fingers opened to take it, and down dropped the midwife's gold wedding ring.

From As You Like It, *by William Shakespeare*
                    At first the infant,
Mewling and puking in the nurse's arms.
Then the whining school-boy with his satchel
And shining morning face, creeping like a snail
Unwillingly to school . . .

Letter to his mother from Frederick Reynolds aged about seven, after two days at Westminster School, London 1750
My dear, dear Mother,
If you don't let me come home, I die.
I am all over ink, and my fine clothes have been spoilt – I have been tost in a blanket, and seen a ghost.
I remain, my dear, dear mother

Your most dutiful and most
　　Unhappy son,
　　Freddy
P.S. Remember me to father.

Mrs Thrale from Diary 1777
Dr Collier used to say speaking of Parental Affection that one
loved one's Children in Anticipation, one hopes they will one
day become useful, estimable, and amiable Beings – one
cannot love lumps of Flesh continued he, and they are nothing
better during Infancy.

*Margaret Leveson aged 6, East Scotland 1842 for the Parlia-
mentary Commission inquiry into the state of children in mines
and manufactories*
Been down at coal-carrying six weeks: makes ten to fourteen
rakes a day; carries full 56 pounds of coal in a wooden backit.
The work is na guid; it is so very sair.

The Giddy Girl, 1899
Miss Helen was always too giddy to heed
What her mother had told her to shun;
For frequently, over the street in full speed,
She would cross where the carriages run.
And out she would go to a very deep well
To look at the water below:
How naughty! To run to a dangerous well,
Where her mother forbade her to go!
One morning intending to take but one peep,
Her foot slipped away from the ground;
Unhappy misfortune! The water was deep,
And giddy Miss Helen was drowned.

*'What parents say' Toot Hill Comprehensive School, Bingham,
Nottinghamshire 1979*
Isn't it time you thought about bed?
It must be somewhere.
You speak to him Harold, he won't listen to me
Who do you think I am?
You'd better ask your father
It's late enough as it is

Don't eat with your mouth open
In this day and age
Did anyone ask your opinion?
I remember when I was a boy
And after all we do for you
You're not talking to your school friends now you know
Why don't you do it the proper way?
I'm only trying to tell you
What did I just say?
Now, wrap-up warm
B.E.D. spells bed
Sit up straight and don't gobble your food
For the five hundredth time
Don't let me ever see you do that again
Have you made your bed?
Can't you look further?
Have you done your homework?
Because I say so
Don't come those fancy ways here
Any more and you'll be in bed
My, haven't you grown
Some day I won't be here, and then you'll see
A chair's for sitting on
You shouldn't need telling at your age
Want, want, want, that's all you ever say.

Macleod's lullaby

This is one of many lullabies to the son of Macleod, an ancient song from the Highlands of Scotland. The songs and stories told then were all about ghosts and fairies, birds and beasts, seals and fishes and about what all these said to one another before the sins of men rendered them speechless. Macleod's baby was so beautiful that the fairy folk wanted to steal him. They often came to see him, coddle him, and sing lullabies but he was his parents' darling and he was the centre of their existence in all they did.

This perhaps describes the absolute love of a parent for a child.

Thou art my harp of melody,
My lovely lute,
Thou art my sweet lyre,
My cattle on sheiling,

My white sheep,
My bleating goats,
My milking cow,
My horned flock,
Thou art my harp of melody,
My smiling lute,
Thou art my sweet harp,
My winsome love.

Chapter 2

Definitions of play therapy

Play therapy is a way of helping troubled children cope with their distress, using play as the medium of communication between child and therapist. The method is based on the central assumption that play is the place where children first recognise the separateness of what is 'me' and 'not me' and begin to develop a relationship with the world beyond the self. It is the child's way of making contact with their environment.

Definitions of play therapy will be determined by the perspectives of the person describing the process. My discourse is from the perspective of a play therapist with an interest in the imaginative play of children and adults. My definitions have a specific quality related to my professional experience but much of my understanding of children and my profession is derived from the dominant cultural image of the 'normal' child. It is important to recognise that there is no one 'truth' about play therapy but a number of perspectives based on the learning, experience and expertise of the presenter.

Meldrum (1996) states that exploration of theory arises out of the practice of play therapy. She describes a play therapist working with abused children. What emerges from practice with abused children is a loss of identity, a loss of the sense of self and often a distorted attachment to the perpetrator, stronger and more demanding because desperate, than a secure attachment in a loving relationship. The child who has no sense of self cannot separate her or himself from the person who is abusing them. This knowledge about the effects of abuse should inform the practice of the play therapist and will influence the way the process of the therapy supports the client. She emphasises that theory should underpin practice rather than be imposed on practice.

The centrality of play in play therapy

There are general principles that apply to all play therapy interventions and do not depend on a particular mode of working. The key process is the use of mostly imaginative play that takes place within a relationship between the child and therapist. What Winnicott called 'playing in the presence of someone'. The child who comes for play therapy will be actively playing and replaying complex environmental issues and trying to cast them into manageable forms. When the play is shared with the therapist who is non-judgemental, then the negative effects of anger, distress–sadness, or shame–humiliation can be relieved through the play within the relationship.

When children play imaginatively, in whatever context, they create a fictional world, which can be a way of making sense of their real world. Vandenberg (1986) states that to be human and live in a meaningful way within a culture requires that we live in and through a very sophisticated abstract system that is largely imaginary. Our social relationships and understanding of our world and our culture depend on our understanding of these systems of communication both verbal and non-verbal. Jokes, irony, skills of persuasion, figures of speech, are all part of this system as well as non-verbal signals and signs like eye contact, smiling. Sometimes children have not learnt all these complex functions and that can be part of their shame and humiliation. We can all remember phrases used by adults, which puzzled us as small children. 'He's got a frog in his throat', what on earth did that mean?

If we examine the skipping rhymes of children we can see how aspects of culture and personal relationships are learnt through play.

House to Let (nineteenth century)
House to let –
Apply within;
As I go out
My neighbour comes in

House to let –
Apply within;
A woman put out
For drinking gin.

House to let –
Apply within;

A woman put out
For showing her thing.

House to Let (twentieth century)
House to let –
Apply within,
As I go out
A lady comes in.

My Big Red Ball
My big red *ball*
Went over the *wall*
I told my *mum*
She skelpt my *bum.*
B.U.M.

Over the Mountain
Over the mountain,
Over the sea
Johnny broke a window
And blamed it on me.

I told my ma
My ma told my dad,
Johnny got a leathering
Ha! Ha! Ha!

Policeman Policeman
Policeman, policeman, don't blame *me,*
Blame that boy behind the *tree,*
He stole sugar and he stole *tea,*
Policeman, policeman don't blame *me.*

I'm a Little Orphan Girl
I'm a little orphan girl
My mother she is dead:
My father is a drunkard
And won't buy me my bread.

I sit upon the window sill
To hear the organ play

And think of my dear mother
Who's dead and far away.

Ding, dong my castle bell
Farewell to my mother
Bury me in the old churchyard
Beside my elder brother.

My coffin shall be white
Six little angels by my side
Two to sing and two to play
And two to carry my soul away.

Bluebells and Cockle-shells
Bluebells and cockle-shells
Eevie, ivy, o-over
Dr Brown is a very good man
He teaches the children all he can:
First to read and then to write,
Eevie, ivy, I pop out.

The Beatles' School
In the Beatles' *school*
In Liver*pool*
They learn their *yea yea yea*

As an adult, I am reminded of the way we might tease people
who find difficulties with the complexities of subtle communication. An example of this is contained in the TV programme *The
Vicar of Dibley*. At the end of each episode, the vicar tells a joke to
her verger whose literal view of the world means that she doesn't
really understand the meaning of the joke. While the vicar is
sympathetic, she knows her verger won't understand the joke and
that confusion becomes another joke in the kind of way we laugh
at children's misunderstandings. While it is a comedy programme
the relationship between vicar and verger seems to meet the need of
the vicar to define her own identity, as a patient and caring but
superior person. There is a moral here for the play therapist who
might also be using the child's vulnerability to bolster their own
confidence rather than nurturing the child's independence. These
are issues explored in training programmes.

Troubled children often feel they are responsible for what has happened to them. They feel worthless and stupid. Their anxiety about being stupid and not understanding the adult world is the theme of many folk tales. Telling stories to children within a therapeutic relationship can help them see that others share their concerns. This can be important in the development of the relationship between child and therapist. One of my favourite stories about feeling stupid (is it ADHD?) is called *A Pottle o' Brains*.

A Pottle o' Brains

Once in these parts, and not so long ago, there was a boy who wanted to buy a pottle o' brains, for he was always getting into scrapes because of his foolishness, and being laughed at by everyone.

Folk told him he could get everything he liked from the wise woman that lived on the top of the hill, and dealt in potions and herbs and spells and things. She could even tell the future. So the boy asked his mother if he could seek the old woman and buy a pottle o' brains.

'Yes you can,' said his mother 'you are in great need of them and if I die who would take care of such a fool as you who has no more idea of looking after yourself than a new-born baby. But mind your manners when you speak to her because such wise folk are quickly displeased.'

So off he went, after his tea, and there she was, sitting by the fire, stirring a big pot.

'Good evening, missis,' he says, 'it's a fine night.'

'Aye,' says she and went on stirring.

'It'll maybe rain,' says he and fidgets from one foot to the other.

'Maybe,' says she.

'And happen it won't,' says he and looks out of the window.

'Happen,' says she.

And he scratched his head and twisted his cap.

'Well,' says he, 'I can't mind nothing else about the weather, but let me see, the crops are getting on fine.'

'Fine,' says she.

'And-the-beasts-is-fattening,' says he.

'They are,' says she.

'And, and, and,' then he comes to a stop.

'I reckon we'll tackle business now having done the polite like. Have you any brains to sell?'

'That depends,' says she, 'if you want a king's brains, or a soldier's brains or a schoolmaster's brains, I dinna keep them.'

'Oh no,' says he, 'just ordinary brains, same as everyone has around here, something clean, common like.'

'Aye so,' says the old woman, 'I might manage that if you'll help yourself.'

'How do I do that missis?' says he.

'Bring me the heart of the thing you like best of all, and I'll tell you where to get your pottle o' brains, but you'll have to read me a riddle, so as I can see you've brought the right thing, and if your brain is about you.'

'But,' says he scratching his head, 'how can I do that?'

'That's not for me to say. Find out for yourself my lad.'

So the boy went back home and told his mother what had happened.

'I reckon I'll have to kill the pig,' says he, 'for I like fat bacon better than anything.'

So he killed the pig and next day set off for the old woman's cottage.

'Good-day,' he said, 'I've brought you the heart of the thing I love best.'

'Aye so,' said she and looked at him through her spectacles. 'Tell me this then, what runs without feet?'

He scratched his head and thought and thought but couldn't tell.

'Go thy ways,' said the old woman, 'you haven't fetched me the right thing yet.'

So off the boy went to tell his mother but as he got to his house, out came folk running to tell him his mother was dying. When he got in, his mother smiled because she thought he had his brains and then she died.

The boy was very sad because he remembered how kind his mother had been to him and how she had looked after him so well and put up with his foolishness.

Then he realised that his mother was the one he loved the best but he couldn't cut out her heart to bring to the old woman.

So he put his mother into a sack and carried her body to the old woman's cottage.

'Good-day missis,' says he. 'I think I've fetched the right thing this time.'

'Maybe,' said the old woman, 'but read me this, now what's yellow and shining but isn't gold?'

He scratched his head, and thought but couldn't tell.

'Thou hast not hit the right thing yet,' said the old woman.

'You are more foolish than I thought.'

The boy left and sat down by the roadside.

'I've lost the only two things I care for. What else can I find to buy a pottle o' brains?' And he began to cry.

And up came a girl who lived nearby and asked him what had happened and he told her about the old woman and the pottle o' brains and that he was now alone in the world.

'Well I wouldn't mind looking after you,' said the girl. 'People like you make good husbands.'

They got married and decided to wait a bit before going to see the old woman again.

The boy and girl were very happy together and after a while, the boy told the girl that she was now the person he liked best of everything.

'But I'm not going to cut out your heart for a pottle o' brains.'

'I'm glad to hear it,' said the girl. 'You take me to see the old woman and I'll help you read the riddles.'

'I reckon they are too hard for womenfolk,' said he.

'Well let's see now. Tell me the first.'

'What runs without feet?'

'Why water,' says she.

'And what is yellow and shining and not gold?'

'Why the sun,' says she.

'That's right,' says he, 'come we'll go to the old woman.'

So off they went.

The old woman was sitting outside twining straws.

'Good-day missis,' says he, 'I reckon I've fetched the right thing at last.'

The wise woman looked at them both.

'Canst tell me what that is as has first no legs, and then two legs, and ends with four legs?'

And the boy scratched his head but couldn't tell.

And the girl whispered in his ear.

'It's a tadpole.'

The boy told the old woman who nodded her head.

'That's right, and you have your pottle o' brains already.'
'Where be they?' he asked searching in his pockets.
'In your wife's head,' says she.
So they went home together and he never wanted to buy a pottle o' brains again, for his wife had enough for both.

Play worlds and reality worlds

The child who comes to play therapy chooses to play in their own way with the toys, objects and other materials which the therapist offers. The connections between the play world and reality worlds may not be evident. We live in both worlds. The importance of imaginative play for the child is to create a world in which they are a powerful presence and have mastery over what they have created. In my work with 'looked after' children, I have noted that many boys begin their play by placing toy cars in car parks or on the motorway. They make patterns with the cars, which drive themselves; no humans appear to damage the perfect symmetry of the patterns the cars make. They are in control of a world made up of cars, not people. This might also be the play of an autistic child who wants some control over a chaotic environment which is hard to understand. The autistic child needs the familiarity of the same cars and the repetition of the patterns and may not be able to move beyond this patterning play.

The 'looked after' child may also repeat the car play, as reassurance of safety in an ever-changing world, but their play might develop to include a simple narrative about crashes, traffic queues, getting out of the car park. There is never much connection to the child's reality world in the way of exploring life narratives in a linear way, but the constant repetition of manoeuvring the cars, which are objects of desire, gives the child a world of safety and predictability. Perhaps it is how the child daydreams to cope with constant change.

This kind of play alleviates suffering for the child, they feel safe, contained and in control of the world they have created. This does not mean they are safe enough to change their perspective on their life experiences. The child is choosing to use the time with the therapist to feel safe and secure because that is what the child needs to do. It is often hard for the therapist to accept these activities without trying to push the child to more imaginative play or to make interpretations with which the child will not connect. The difficulty for the therapist is boredom with the repetition!

Sometimes the child is struggling to develop more imaginative play but hasn't the language or the confidence to tell a story to the therapist. At this point, I offer to tell stories to the child if they want to listen. There is no better way to learn how to tell a story than by listening to one being told to you and you alone.

There are many funny folk tales about the adventures of Jack, the boy who kills giants or goes into the world to seek his fortune. He is also a hero in travellers' tales and his adventures are much enjoyed by many 'looked after' children who feel they have to cope without the nurture of parent figures. This is one such tale.

Jack and the Ghosts

Once there was a lad called Jack, and as he was passing a churchyard at night he saw three ghosts fighting.

He hurried past, but the ghosts came after him and brought him back to settle their disputes.

They were well pleased with the way he settled it and they gave him three presents – a piece of dough, and a needle and some cloth.

They told him they would be of great use to him, for they were magic.

So Jack went on his way until he came to a town and the first shop he saw was a baker's shop. It was filled with ancient cakes, a hundred and fifty years old or so.

He went into the shop but there was nothing fit to eat there and the baker told him that the queen had ordered him to bake a cake, but he had only a pound of flour in the place.

'Leave it to me,' said Jack and he went alone into the bakehouse and said to the dough 'Do your work.'

And the dough set to and baked itself into a most beautiful cake, and cakes and bread and pies until the shop was full.

The baker was delighted and begged Jack to stay with him but Jack wouldn't stay.

He went on to the next shop and that was a tailor's full of old ragged clothes.

The tailor was in despair because the queen had ordered him to make her a most beautiful frock.

Jack set the piece of cloth to work and it made the most beautiful frock embroidered with gold.

The tailor took it to the queen and begged Jack to stay with him but Jack wouldn't stay.

The next shop he came to was a shoemaker's and the shoemaker had been ordered to make grand shoes for the queen.

And here the needle set to and stitched and stitched until it had made shoes for the queen and the princes and the whole court besides.

Then the queen sent out a notice that she wanted the whole palace done up.

And Jack presented himself with his needle and his cloth and did up the palace so there was nothing to equal it.

And the queen gave him a great reward.

But about this time pigs began to go missing from the royal pigsties and for one reason and another they began to suspect Jack.

So they put a watch on him and one night they caught Jack carrying a pig **in** through the door instead of **out**.

So they married him to the king's daughter and they lived happily all their days.

The End.

Varieties of imaginative play

There are three kinds of imaginative play, which can be present in a play therapy intervention.

1. *Embodiment play.* This is the play of the young infant exploring the world through the senses, using play materials like play-doh, slime, clay and paint. This is the play of the young infant defining the world by discovering where their body ends and the rest of the world begins. It is the child's way of expanding their world.
2. *Projective play* happens when the child discovers the world outside themselves through toys, dolls and other play objects. The child uses these objects to represent other objects, so a doll becomes a baby and a stick becomes a sword. Through these objects children can explore alternative stories through pretend play and storymaking. Toys and objects assist the child in externalisation and help the child to separate from a problem and expand their perspectives.

3. *Role-play* occurs when a child begins playing themselves in a familiar situation and then pretends to be someone else. The process of drama allows transformation from everyday reality into dramatic reality. These transformational experiences create shifts for the child and are experienced on a bodily kinaesthetic level.

Developmental psychologists describe these modes of play as part of the child's social play. Dunn (1993) states that babies play an active part in interactional games like peek-a-boo and later hide and seek, enjoying the give and take of the play. Dunn defines this play as two or more individuals working towards a mutual goal, with alternation of turns and repetition of actions.

Dunn found that in the years between early infancy and nursery school, babies as young as eight months are able to respond to the playful moods of their siblings, frequently imitating their actions. At 18 months the child is actively imitating their older siblings' pretend play, co-operating and imitating sequences of actions. This ability of children to co-operate in pretend play is one of the most striking features of the period between infancy and school.

Dunn's research also indicates that during the second and third years, children not only take one role in a joint game with siblings but also are able to reverse roles. The child begins this role-play at the sibling's suggestion, but by the end of the second year, the younger child is able to take the initiative. This pretend play involves the capacity of the child to share a pretend framework with another person, to co-ordinate pretend actions, to be able to act as another person or a thing and also mutually explore social roles and rules.

Meldrum (1996) emphasises that all new skills, materials and resources are set inside an ecological context of the social environment. She states that while it is perfectly possible to observe the infant looking at its own limbs moving and because it seems to be enjoying the activity, for us to label the activity 'early play' we must be aware that we are giving an adult meaning to a set of behaviours that are species-specific and part of the development of the human being. She makes the point that it is an adult's meaning we are imposing and the meanings we ascribe to behaviour form part of our own value system influenced by our own experience.

These three modes of playing are present in therapy. Some or all may appear in an intervention. Some children prefer a particular mode of play and will stay in that mode throughout the therapy. Many neglected children will want to use embodied, sensory play as their means of expression because they missed so much nurture as infants. Children who do not feel safe enough to explore their family difficulties may also seek consolation in embodied play and use the play as a beginning search for identity.

The car play of boys is a form of projective play when the cars and the pattern they make express safety. Perhaps the child is learning to construct a symbolic world, which has the conventions and rules for cars, and in this pretend world everybody keeps the rules. Sometimes the play appears to hold little meaning for the child other than a repetitive activity expressing a sense of helplessness. John always used cars to express his lack of attachment and sense of isolation as he drifted in care from placement to placement. At first his play was setting cars in a car park but later he was able to develop this play a little. This is a typical story.

John's Car Story
All of the cars are in the town.
They are coming for Christmas shopping.
All the cars are driven by Fat Controllers.
[*I ask if there are any families in this town.*]
There are no families at all.
They are all at home because they are not well.
Because it is snowing.
That is why the Fat Controllers have to do all the shopping.
All the families made lists.
There are lots and lots of cars and they all park up in the car park.
The End.

I think John's life was organised by Fat Controllers, including myself. The world he constantly describes is a place that seems to lack human interaction but things get done by Fat Controllers through lists. That was his experience of being cared for by social workers and foster carers; he didn't feel connected, presents appeared from lists, things happened to you that were beyond your control or understanding. He felt helpless.

Sometimes the expressions of loss and grief are very powerfully expressed. This boy had been waiting four years for an adoptive family.

The Broken Heart
Once upon a time there was a broken heart.
It didn't belong to anybody
And it was dead.
With no hope of coming alive again
This heart has no name.
Because hearts never have names in the world.
They are just hearts.
These are tears for the heart.
[*He painted tears all over the page.*]
The End.

Projective play can also be complex storymaking, which can be narrated with the toys and objects or develop into role-play and become a dramatic presentation. When I play with children who want to dramatise a story or characters, I will participate if asked by the child. We go through the story and the roles first so I play what the child requests, through my questions about the role. If I think that my role is not appropriate and will reinforce abusive patterns I won't embody that person but suggest that the child plays out the story with dolls. For example, a child said 'You be the rapist and I'll be the little girl.' I said that part was too scary for me to play but if she wanted she could make the play with dolls. This is the way that children negotiate role-playing when they are together in a group so they don't feel rejected when a role is refused. We've all heard children say, 'I don't want to be the princess' or such like, as they negotiate play with other children.

Aesthetic distance through imaginative play

When the child plays with toys and other materials and narrates a story with the objects or dramatises the play the child is distanced from their reality world. Child and therapist enter into an imaginary world of play together and create an alliance of distance to explore what is created in play. It is a paradoxical process because we can come closer to the issues that concern us through the distance created by the processes in the play. Grainger (1990) states that we distance ourselves (or art distances itself because this is an artistic process) in order to be engaged with and involved in, the thing that we are standing back from. Jennings (1998) considers that we live in two realities. We have the reality of our perception of our everyday concrete world and our forays into our imagination. She states that her definition of maturation (she is writing as a dramatherapist) is the capacity to distinguish everyday and dramatic reality and to be able to move in and out of each appropriately.

Some inexperienced therapists want to connect the world of the imagination to the child's reality world through rather simplistic 'interpretations' of the narratives the child presents in therapy. Play and stories in play are symbolic representations and as such have a multiplicity of meanings, which cannot be encapsulated in literal cross-references.

In this way play therapy is similar to all artistic forms and, like a line of poetry, the meaning is most effective in the imagery. Gerard Manley Hopkins wrote,

> As kingfishers catch fire, dragonflies draw flame
> As tumbled over rims in roundy wells
> Stones ring . . .

The levels of meaning rest within the language of the poem. We can discuss the poem together as the child and therapist can discuss the play and narratives in the session but it is most important to keep the focus of discussion within the framework of the play. If the child senses that the therapist is trying to use what is played for some adult purpose of extracting information from the child then play becomes inhibited and the child will then start to play what he thinks the adult is seeking and creativity becomes stunted. The dangers of making interpretations of the reality world from the play world are many. It might give the therapist a sense of security to think that burying a small figure in a sand tray means that the child has been sexually abused but there is no evidence to support this assertion for all children.

Sometimes the imaginary worlds created by children seem very fearful places. Perhaps for the powerless this has to be so if they are to be heard at all.

Here are some examples:

The River of Blood
This is a scary place and the king of the place is the Devil.
He has a battle in the River of Blood
And everybody gets sucked up except the Devil.

He eats everything trapped in the river.
He dives in and out of the blood.
The river is made up of the blood of the creatures he has eaten.
He was a very good boy
But a wizard called him
And turned him into the Devil.
The End

The Horrible Monster

One day Mouse Monster made a huge stew of people.
Just different coloured people.
They were alive when he put them in the stew.
It was a bloody stew.
He ate and ate and ate.
He loved it.
He wasn't sick.
All the people said:
'Help, I'm getting eaten.'
He made a lot of noise when he chewed people.
He was a most unpleasant person.
There was blood everywhere.
Even in the pond.
Help, help, help croaked the frog.
The End.

The Wobbly People

All the wobbly people live on one side of the hole.
And the snakes live on the other side of the hole.
They are not nice.
None of them are nice.
They don't fight.
They just kill people.
They kill by frightening them.
They are scary and they are lonely.
They play games, lonely, scary, killing people.
They live in the hole.
They like it in the hole because nobody notices them.
They don't get sad.
Sometimes they get angry and kill people.
Sometimes they get mad and kill people.
They are mad because they didn't kill them.

They are mad sick, not mad angry.
They feel sick in the holidays because they don't like each
other.
The snakes are the horrible people in town.
They don't get sent away.
They stay in the hole.
So nobody takes them away in the country.
The End

However, sometimes circumstances change, the river of blood
becomes a safer place.

The River
There was once a river.
It was a nice place.
And a family of frogs lived there.
The river was pink and warm.
Sometimes they sat on top of the river
And sometimes they hid
Because they were playing hide and seek.
They hid when the weather got cold.
When people came they showed off on top of the river.
They didn't swim
But they danced and croaked
And people thought they were really beautiful.
In the frog family there was just a mum who was blue
There were three children and a country to live in.
They all liked each other.
Sometimes they had arguments.
But mostly not.
The End.

Child/therapist relationship

The relationship between child and therapist should be collaboration and a shared exploration of the issues agreed when therapist,
carers and child first meet. There is always an initial meeting with
referrer, carers, therapist and child to discuss and share information. The therapist can explain to the child and the adults
present what can be offered and how the sessions are organised.
Sometimes the length of the intervention is constrained by events in

the life of the child, or the finance available, and it is important to be clear about what can be done from the very first meeting. Practical details must be clear, for example, who brings and collects the child, where will the meetings take place and is the accommodation booked for continuity.

It is important that the child is clear about the organisation of the sessions, how the play will be conducted, and the reasons for the intervention. Informed consent is very difficult to achieve with a young child, so the therapist must be very clear in the way the child is told about the sessions. The child should be given time to consider whether they want to participate in the therapy because unlike most adults the decision about the need for therapy is initially made by adults rather than the child herself.

West (1992 (1996)) describes the 'Being' skills of the play therapist, which I think are critical for the relationship. She lists:

the ability to get on, and communicate with children
genuineness
authenticity
positive regard
non-possessive warmth
accurate empathy
reliability,
respect for, and non-exploitation of, children.

I would add being creative in play, which enables the child to feel that their play is respected as well as their person.

The play therapist's knowledge base

The key area of knowledge for the play therapist is an understanding of all the modes of imaginative play, not just through watching, but also by participating in all forms of play. The impact of making a painting using finger-paints or using figures in a sand tray to tell a story, can be strongly emotional and leaves an impact. This must be so otherwise we would not use the medium in therapy. The therapist needs to experience these play processes as themselves to understand their impact before asking a child to play. This is why training is imperative for the therapist.

In play therapy the therapist may be the listener to the child's play or participate in dramatic play at the child's request. It is very important that the therapist constantly plays to maintain their own levels of creativity and skill and is comfortable with play as an activity for all, rather than something that only children do which they grow out of with age.

Sometimes, when I am training I notice that some adults find it difficult to play as themselves and pretend they are children as though play is something adults don't do. There seems to be a refusal to explore their own feelings through play and I wonder why they want to impose a form on children that they are unable to use for themselves.

The therapist needs to know about the theory and practice of play therapy and recognise that ideas change and develop so the knowledge is not static. This knowledge should be critically evaluated at all times. What might have been helpful to the middle-class child in 1930's Hampstead, might not have much connection for the child in 2002 'looked after' in the care system, and play activities for a child refugee from Somalia, for example, will have their own cultural resonances.

The play therapist works as part of a team and in that context can offer unique knowledge and understanding. Basic knowledge for the play therapist should include the following:

- The play therapist works in a social environment where issues of race, gender, disability and power impact on the work.
- A knowledge of child and adolescent studies, exploring and encompassing sociology, philosophy, psychology and anthropology is necessary.
- Key themes for play therapists to explore through academic studies are the difficulties of parenting, the effects of loss, abuse, multiple placements and other traumatic events on the lives of children and adolescents.
- A knowledge of childhood illnesses, difficulties and disabilities that impact on the life of the child is needed.
- Ethical and legal issues relating to children and families and the practice of play therapy are an essential knowledge base for the professional practitioner.
- A knowledge of other therapies that can be offered to children and families can help the therapist determine which interventions will be most useful for the child. Sometimes adults will be using one form of therapy while the child has play therapy and

it is important to have an understanding of other modalities that would support family members.

- The therapist needs to know her/himself so critical knowledge is self-understanding through personal therapy that is mandatory in all training programmes.

Outcomes of play therapy

When the child, carers, referrers and therapist first meet, the issues that bring the child to therapy are explored. From this information a formulation about the intervention is suggested so that the meaning of the meetings and the eventual outcomes emerge. The formulation may shift as the therapy progresses but the therapy is referenced to the formulation. This can include the number of sessions available, meetings with carers and/or referrers and final discussion of the outcomes with child and adults.

So, for example, a child who has been sexually abused may be coping well, able to talk to carers, but still have difficulties at bedtime. So the intervention might be to help lessen the anxiety about bedtime. The therapist might talk through bedtime routines with the child and carers. I often ask the child about the setting in the bedroom. Sometimes the gap under the bed is the fear or flapping curtains. Practical remedies here can help the carers feel useful rather than helpless in the face of the child's distress.

The symbolic nature of the play would help the child feel safe. The therapist's capacity to listen to the stories presented in play, could lead to a shift in the perspectives of the child about the abuse they had experienced. New coping strategies could emerge and this could then increase the confidence of the child's carers who would be more empowered to help the child.

Mary was eight when she came to see me. She came with her mother and younger sister who knew about the abuse she had experienced from the partner of a babysitter. The abuse had happened some time ago but Mary found it difficult to talk about the details of what happened with her mother because her mother became distressed. We agreed in the first meeting that it would be helpful for Mary to come and play and also talk about the details of what had happened. Mary made one rule: that her mother was not to ask about what happened in the sessions with me. Mary's mother agreed to this and as trust developed between us was able to joke about it. She said that she would like to be a fly on the

ceiling to see what went on as we played. But she was very con-
scientious about the agreement and never asked Mary to discuss
our meetings.

In play therapy, Mary played about issues of power and
helplessness. Trust developed between us because Mary controlled
all the play and what we spoke about before we began to play
together. In the fifth session, before we played together, Mary was
able to discuss the disgust she felt about the genitals of the perpetrator. That was the issue that had preoccupied her thoughts.
Humour was one way we defused this anxiety and we had many
giggles about bodies and rude rhymes were repeated with relish.
From that session Mary was able to talk freely and in her play the
heroes became more assertive in power struggles.

It had been agreed that Mary could determine the number of
sessions she felt she needed and after eight meetings she said she
was satisfied. Our final evaluation with Mary, her mother and
sister, was that Mary was more relaxed at home, there was less
fighting between the sisters, school work was improving as Mary
could concentrate better, and her mother felt less anxious about
her daughter. The confidentiality of the sessions was maintained
and Mary's mother was happy to support this as she could see that
Mary was much more confident in her relationships with adults
and her peers. There might be further difficulties at a later time but
for now the family considered that they had achieved their goals.

Ten parameters of play therapy: a checklist

Dighton (2001) describes ten key assumptions that form the
parameters of play therapy. This is a helpful checklist for the new
therapist before meeting a client.

1. Children's experiences that relate to problems, difficulties or
   conflicts gravitate towards expression.
2. That the associations between the expression and the experiences that relate to problems, difficulties or conflicts may be
   known or unknown.
3. That therapeutic change is not premised on the awareness of
   the association between the expression and the experiences that
   relate to problems, difficulties or conflicts.
4. That children's natural and instinctive medium of expression is
   play.

5. That an integral element of play is its symbolic distance.
6. That symbolic distance enables children to safely express their feelings, thoughts, beliefs and attitudes surrounding their life experiences that relate to problems, difficulties or conflicts.
7. That these life experiences are expressed, explored and made sense of through the dynamic interaction between the child and therapist.
8. That these interactions are a process that takes place within the context of a clearly defined therapeutic relationship, therapeutic space and therapeutic contract.
9. That the therapeutic process can enable children both to actively change their perspectives on their life experiences and to alleviate suffering related to their life experiences.
10. That such changes of perspectives may translate into changes of behaviour, cognition, affect, attitude and/or beliefs.

Thus, play therapy is a collaborative inquiry into the child's world that is contained within the therapeutic relationship primarily between therapist, child and significant others. The language of this inquiry is predominantly symbolic, allowing the child to explore their life experiences through such symbolic communication.

Conclusions

In this chapter it has been determined that definitions of play therapy will differ according to the knowledge base, experience, profession and social environment of the person who presents the definition. So a description of play therapy from a clinical psychologist might differ from the definition of a dramatherapist or a child psychiatrist.

However, there are key concepts that need to be addressed by all play therapists for the protection of the clients.

• We are helping troubled children.
• The medium of communication is play.
• The play is symbolic.
• The relationship between child and therapist is one of mutuality.
• The therapist is trained for the work.
• There is a formulation of the issues, and outcomes are defined at the beginning of the intervention.

Games for therapists starting to play

Many children's games have a deep symbolic meaning and represent aspects of the lived experience within the structure and meaning of the play. Perhaps that is why the playing sometimes ends in tears!

Try these for yourself.

First, beginning, embodied play. What do I look like?

Two face rhymes

Bo Peeper
Bo Peeper
Nose Dreeper
Chin Chopper
White Lopper
Red Rag
And Little Gap

Here Sits the Lord Mayor
Here sits the Lord Mayor,
Here sits his two men (eyes)
Here sits the cocadoodle (right cheek)
Here sits the hen (left cheek)
Here sits the little chickens (tip of nose)
Here they run in (mouth)
Chinchopper, chinchopper,
Chinchopper chin.

Hide and seek

The feeling of losing someone and the process of finding them again or skills at hunting and chasing are what we learn in this game. The person who is 'it' shuts their eyes, and counts possibly to a hundred or as follows:

'*Five, ten, double ten,*
Five, ten, fifty
Five, ten, double ten,
Five, ten, a hundred.'
(Not quite accurate but is repeated again and again.)

Everybody hides.
The seeker finishes the count and calls out

> '*Look out, look out, the fox is about,*
> *And he is coming to find you.*'

Or

> '*The cock doth crow, the wind doth blow,*
> *I don't care whether you are hidden or no,*
> *I'm coming.*'

The seeker goes to find those who are hiding.
Those who are found can warn those still hidden

> '*Keep in, keep in, wherever you are,*
> *The cat's a-coming to find you.*'

If arguments or boredom stop the game you call:

> '*Allee-ins, not playing*'

Or

> '*Olly, olly in*'

Or

> '*Come oot, come oot, wherever you are,*
> *The game's a bogie.*'

In spring there is Marbles or Bools. Marbles are beautiful objects and you might lose them in this game. This is projective play with objects.

> *Stakie or Ringie or Daikie*
> Scratch or chalk a ring on the ground.
> All the players put in an equal amount of marbles.
> Everybody stands about four or five feet away.
> Each rolls a marble and the nearest to the ring gets first plonk at the marbles inside.

If the player knocks one marble out of the ring he keeps it.
If the player knocks two out before any of the others say
'*Knock out two put one back,*'
The player says '*Knock out two put **none** back,*'
The player keeps both.
The same applies to three or more marbles.
When you mss, the next person gets a chance at plonking.
When all the Daik (deck) is finished a fresh game is started.

And a game for role-play. How to escape the monster? In this game
you run away. A good strategy!

What's the Time Mr Wolf?
One person is Mr Wolf.
He walks along the road jauntily.
The rest of the group are as close behind as they dare.
They call after him
'What's the time Mr Wolf?'
He replies in a frightening voice
'Seven o'clock,'
or any other time.
He keeps on walking.
The group call again
'What's the time Mr Wolf?'
This goes on and the group continue to pester Mr Wolf
In the end Mr Wolf shouts
'Dinner time.'
And Mr Wolf rushes after the group
Who run screaming back to the starting place.
If anyone is caught they are Mr Wolf for the next game.

Chapter 3

Models of play therapy

There are a variety of approaches to play therapy, largely determined by the context in which the intervention takes place, the professional and theoretical perspective of the therapist and the needs of the child.

In this chapter I will explore three modes of working; non-directive play therapy, focused play therapy and my own approach, which is collaborative play therapy. I have not included psycho-analytic modes of working, as this is the remit of the child psychotherapist rather than the play therapist. While aspects of these theories are explored in the training of play therapists they are not the central focus of the practice of the majority of trained play therapists in Britain.

Carroll (2001) describes the practice of play therapy as on a continuum from non-directive to focused techniques with a prescribed process and defined goals. The non-directive focus emphasises the child's ability to select those materials which make most sense to him or her, and to use them to explore internal and external experiences and resolve difficulties in their own way and their own time.

She considers that most therapists adhere to child-centred principles in the sense that children are given real choices on undertaking any exercises suggested. Many therapists also introduce more focused techniques, for example, interventions designed to promote a general release of feeling to those with more specific goals such as helping bereaved children explore the meaning of loss.

There seems to be some confusion in Carroll's description between a focus for play therapy, techniques of play, and information-sharing between child and therapist. There must be a reason for all interventions, which should be clear for the child, so in that way all play therapy is focused. It would be a deceit to play with a child without their understanding of the purpose of play therapy.

Dighton (2001) describes three approaches:

1. Child directed in which the therapist is non-directive in approach allowing the child to direct the agenda, focus and timing of the play therapy. Such an approach is predicated upon child-centred perspectives and has emerged from the humanistic psychology movement and Axline's non-directive play therapy.
2. Therapist-directed approach in which the therapist is directive in approach and formulates the agenda, focus and timing of the play therapy. This approach is influenced by structured and directive interventions emerging from areas such as cognitive behavioural therapy, filial therapy and social work practice.
3. Collaborative approach in which the therapist utilises both non-directive and directive approaches allowing the child and therapist equal power to direct the agenda, focus and timing of the play therapy. This approach has emerged from narrative therapy, solution focused therapy and family therapy.

I find that these descriptions of methods emphasise psychological processes within therapy with the idea that play therapy emerged from other forms of therapy. They do not explore the meanings of the play itself as a creative and artistic process. In this way, although described as child-centred, the playfulness of play, and the passion and intensity of the experience of playing with some-one, seems to be missing from the descriptions. Play therapy also developed from child drama, child art and other expressive arts in schools and then through the development of the arts as therapy.

Non-directive play therapy

Non-directive play therapy is based on the Rogerian model of psychotherapy which Axline developed into a non-directive model of play therapy.

Wilson, Kendrick and Ryan (1992) describe the central tenet of Rogerian psychotherapy as that individuals have within themselves a basic drive towards health and better functioning and that they possess the ability to solve their problems if offered the opportunity and right climate in which to do so. Rogers saw the therapist's role as being the creation of the right conditions in which this 'self-actualisation' could take place.

The therapist should possess genuiness and authenticity, which means to be themselves as distinct from adopting a role or defensive posture with the client. The therapist also needs qualities of non-possessive warmth, an attitude of caring without becoming overly emotionally involved and accurate empathy with those who are seeking help so that the client feels understood.

Axline incorporates the Rogerian concepts into her model of play therapy and introduced eight basic principles, which are still the major theoretical mainstays for child-centred play therapy.

Axline (1969) describes the principles of the relationship between child and therapist and states that good rapport is established as soon as possible, there is an acceptance of the child as they are, there is a feeling of permissiveness in the relationship to free the child to express their feelings and the therapist is alert to recognise the feeling and reflect back those feelings so the child gains insight into their behaviour. The therapist respects the child's abilities to solve their own problems. The responsibility to make choices and institute change is the child's. The therapist does not attempt to direct the child's actions or conversation in any manner. The therapist does not attempt to hurry the therapy along and the therapist establishes only those limitations that are necessary to anchor the therapy to the world of reality and to make the children aware of their responsibility in the relationship.

West (1992 (1996)) describes the use of these tenets as enabling her to 'feel into' the child, accepting the play and reflecting something about the child's actions and feelings, attune to the child and work with verbal and non-verbal cues. Wilson, Kendrick and Ryan (1992) describe accurate empathy as responding to the deeper content of what is being communicated by the child. The therapist should follow the child's lead and having attended should reflect this understanding back to the child. These reflective comments should be free of blame or criticism. They suggest that the therapist should avoid giving advice and avoid interpretation.

Ryan and Wilson (1996) describe the theoretical underpinning of their work as based on Piaget's broad developmental framework of adaptation. The mental schemas of children who have become emotionally damaged, may have distorted, conflicting components with strongly negative or conflicting schemas about the self and significant others. The child's need to protect themselves may lead to the development of overly accommodating responses such as passivity or regression to less mature levels of functioning.

They consider that symbolic play is a highly assimilative activity for a child and through such play changes can occur. They describe three changes that occur.

1. Thoughts and feelings previously not available to the child are made conscious and given symbolic representation.
2. With the increased symbolic assimilation during therapy the internal organisation of schemas changes and connections with other personal schemas alter.
3. Schemas become more flexible in assimilating new events to past experiences resulting in changes to the child's mental organisation and changes in the child's behaviour.

The ideas and concepts of Rogerian psychotherapy and Axline's development of this into play therapy create a dynamic form of therapy, which has proved very helpful. The qualities required by the therapist are well expressed and this is a helpful model for many children.

However, the non-directive play therapy model does not emphasise the ecological environment in which the child lives. The child is not considered as part of a community, be it family, carers, the school and the wider ecological environment. The focus is on the child's ability to make their own solutions. Some children might find it difficult to establish a relationship with an adult based only on reflection on the adult's part. Such a reflective relationship may be an inhibiting relationship rather than one that frees them to play. When children play with others they expect a participating response as in any communication and the lack of such a response may create further anxiety for the child or push them into inappropriate behaviour to establish a shared interaction.

The assumption that a child can resolve their difficulties without information about the social environment in which they live could be considered questionable in some circumstances. How does a child make sense of abuse, for example, without some adult input?

Focused play therapy

I have described all play therapy as to some extent focused in that the child and therapist meet with an intention to play to resolve issues which are troubling the child. The venue, the choice of toys by the therapist, the age, appearance identity of the therapist, all give a focus to the relationship whether the therapy is called non-directive, focused or collaborative. In all modes of play with the child, the therapist might offer a suggestion such as a theme for a drawing or a game that could be a focus within a session. However, some play therapy interventions stress a medical model and focus on treatment, planning and intervention described in a medical format.

Cognitive-behavioural play therapy

Knell (1995) describes cognitive-behavioural play therapy (CBPT) as incorporating cognitive and behavioural interventions within a play therapy paradigm. These processes also provide a theoretical framework based on cognitive-behavioural principles within a developmental model. The theoretical framework of cognitive therapy is based on the cognitive model of emotional disorders. This model is based on the interplay of cognition, emotions, behaviour and physiology. Disturbed behaviour is considered to be an expression of irrational thinking. Therapy is based on cognitive change. When working with children using this model, interventions focus on helping the child formulate thoughts that would be adaptive to his or her situation, not to make the child think like an adult.

In CBPT there is a greater emphasis on the child's involvement in treatment than in other behavioural therapies for young children. There are six specific properties related to CBPT.

1. CBPT involves the child in treatment through play. The child is an active participant so issues of resistance and non-compliance can be addressed.
2. CBPT focuses on the child's thoughts, feelings, fantasies and environment. In this way it is possible to focus on a combination of issues like soiling, phobia, etc. as well as the child's feelings about the problem.
3. CBPT provides a strategy or strategies for developing more adaptive thoughts and behaviours. The child is taught new strategies for coping with situations and feelings.
4. CBPT is structured, directive and goal-oriented, rather than open-ended. The therapist works with the child and family to set goals and help the child work towards those goals.

5. CBPT incorporates empirically demonstrated techniques. For example modelling through the use of puppets and dolls by the therapist.
6. CBPT allows for an empirical examination of treatment. The techniques used can be evaluated. What treatment, by whom, is the most effective for this individual with that specific problem, under which set of circumstances?

Comparisons are made between non-directive play therapy and CBPT.

Directions and goals

In non-directive play therapy direction is not accepted because it imposes on the child; does not accept the child as he or she is.

In CBPT therapeutic goals are established and the direction towards the goals is the basis of the intervention.

Play materials and activities

In non-directive play therapy materials, the activities and the direction of the play are always selected by the child.

In CBPT both child and therapist select play and materials.

Play as education

In non-directive play therapy education is not appropriate because it is a form of direction.

In CBPT play is used to teach skills and alternative behaviour.

Interpretations/connections

In non-directive play therapy these are not made by the therapist unless the child introduces them first. The therapist communicates unconditional acceptance not interpretation of symbolic play.

In CBPT interpretations/connections are introduced by the therapist. In this way the therapist brings conflict into verbal expression for the child.

Praise

In non-directive play therapy praise should not be used by the therapist. Praise communicates that the therapist does not accept the child as he or she is but rather wants the child to be a certain way.

In CBPT praise is a crucial component. Praise communicates to the child which behaviours are appropriate and which are not. Praise helps children feel good about themselves.

This form of therapy is used with specific difficulties like encopresis, speech and language disorders, fearful children and sexually abused children.

An example of techniques for sexually abused children could include:

• Systematic desensitivisation through drawings and play.
• Contingency management, for example, awarding stars when the child sleeps in his/her own bed.
• Differential reinforcement of other behaviour, for example, I don't like it when you give me a sloppy kiss but I like it when you give me a hug.
• Modelling, when the therapist expresses confused feelings about touching through puppet play.
• Behavioural rehearsal when the therapist coaches the child to use prevention skills through play or puppet scenes.

Kaduson (1997) describes the use of CBPT with children diagnosed with attention deficit hyperactivity disorder (ADHD). The child selects a small toy or transformer and it is that toy which symbolically represents him/her. This toy is used throughout the intervention. Games are developed with the child with specific objectives in mind. The objectives for the child are to increase on-task behaviour, enhance verbalization of feelings, and increase self-control. Later, perhaps, the child would join a social skills group to generalise the newly learnt behaviours.

In CBPT, play seems to be used as a technique and as such is described in very concrete terms. My perception is that the processes of play are used and controlled by the adult rather than the child. It seems to take away from the child its own power to use play to make sense of experience. In CBPT the adult then uses those play processes in a somewhat heavy-handed way to teach behaviour back to the child. The symbolic nature of play is not explored, just teaching through toys, puppets and dramatic play.

However, this can be a useful process if conducted with flair and imagination. I do think the description of the formulation of the issues that are to be addressed and the evaluation of outcomes are important. It is a pity that the language used is so medical in tone as this seems to suggest the therapist as expert and the family as in need of training. To use a definition of Foucault's (1984) this implies an objectification of the subject and in such circumstances power would then rest with the therapist as expert.

Structured group play therapy

O'Connor (1999) describes a system called structured group eco-systemic play therapy which includes components that address cognitive, behavioural, emotional, physical and social aspects of the child's difficulties. The primary function of the group is to improve the child's peer social interactions. The setting where the group met was a room which had three areas, one like a living room, which was reserved for quiet activities and discussion where snacks were served. In this area the children were expected to make verbal contributions to the group process and to comply with basic manners. Another area contained a table and enough chairs for the group. This was used for table games and art projects and in this area the emphasis was on sharing, co-operation and 'product orientation' through the art work. There was also a large empty area in the room, which was used for gross motor activities and games. Co-operation was emphasised in this area.

The therapist selected the toys and materials which were to be used each week. There were storytelling cards, and art materials and later board games. The format of the group sessions was predetermined. The first segment was a directed relaxation exercise; the second segment was eating a snack together and 'talk time', which focused on topics of concern to group members. After 'talk time' came 'activity time' with the therapist selecting the activities and maintaining primary control. The final 15 minutes was free play where the children could choose their own activity.

The role of the play therapist in the group is to create the group, select the activities and within the group to develop and maintain group goals and a treatment plan across group sessions.

The structure of group play therapy is similar to that of a dramatherapy group but the emphasis in dramatherapy would be the development of the creative skills of group members. Jennings (1990) describes this as a creative expressive group with the focus on the undeveloped healthy aspects of people and the function of the group is to encourage the group members to discover their own creative energy.

Jennings (1998) describes dramatherapy for young people as a way to free them from imposed malfunction from adults. Inappropriate roles can be placed on them for which they are not equipped. She states that the child who can play creatively and enact 'self and other' can go a long way towards dealing with life's issues. The development of dramatic strengths enables greater self-healing. She also suggests that children can benefit from rehearsal of future events and dramatisation of an event that has not yet happened is one of the best ways of gaining mastery over fear.

Filial play therapy

This is a brief intervention, which is a combination of play therapy and family therapy. The therapist trains and supervises parents as they conduct special child-centred play therapy sessions with their own children. The sessions are usually conducted at home without the therapist's direct supervision.

The goals of this therapy are to help parents create an accepting, safe environment in which children can express their feelings fully, gain an understanding of their world, solve problems and develop confidence in themselves and their parents. Families who participate are expected to emerge with better communication skills, problem solving and coping skills and stronger family relationships. The therapist instructs the parents in four basic play session skills, structuring, empathic listening, child-centred imaginary play and limit setting. At the end of the training there is a mock play session with the therapist taking the role of the child. This is discussed fully with the parents including skills feedback and anticipation of what to expect from the parents' children.

The parents then begin sessions with the children. The play sessions involve one parent and one child at a time and the sessions can alternate to include all family members. The therapist observes the initial sessions and provides feedback. As parents begin to feel comfortable they conduct sessions at home independently.

The therapist and parents meet from time to time to discuss the sessions and problem solve family issues that arise and generalise the skills beyond the play sessions to everyday life. This therapy is described by Van Fleet (2000) for families with chronic illness.

Much of the literature around focused play therapy, especially CBPT, is written using a medical model with the emphasis on 'illness' and 'cure' and 'treatment'. Play seems to be used as a 'technique' part of the 'treatment' rather than a healing process in its own right. There seems to be a conflict between definitions of play as a process and the uses to which it is put in treatment terms. The control of the play seems to be taken away from the child.

Filial therapy, however, seems an excellent idea and perhaps the creative playing skills of a trained play therapist could help develop the self-confidence of parents.

Collaborative play therapy: the co-construction model

My own approach is one of collaboration between child and therapist where what happens in the sessions is co-constructed between the two. This model is based on social construction theory and narrative therapy, which describe the development of identity as based on the stories we tell about ourselves and the stories others in our environment tell about us. This approach also recognises the fact that the developing child is part of an ecological system, not an isolated individual. These explorations of identity are processed through the developmental play paradigm that incorporates three modes of play, embodied play, progressive or projected play and enactment or role-play, as described in Chapter 2. These theories have also been described by me in earlier books (Cattanach 1994, 1997, 1999).

Social construction theory

This theory states that all ways of understanding are historically and culturally relative, specific to particular cultures and periods of history. Products of that culture and history are dependent on particular social and economic arrangements prevailing in that culture at that time. Knowledge is sustained by social processes and shared versions of knowledge are constructed in the course of our daily lives together. We make use of words in conversations to perform actions in a moral universe. What we define as truth is a product not of objective observation of the world but of the social processes and interactions in which people are constantly engaged with each other.

So child and therapist construct a space and a relationship together where the child can develop a personal and social identity by finding stories to tell about the self and the lived world of that self. The partnership agreement between child and therapist gives meaning to the play as it happens. The stories children tell in therapy are imaginative expressions of what it feels like to live in their real and imagined worlds. The world of stories presented can be mediated by the therapist who can help sort out cognitive confusions present in the play and stories. Sometimes there is a process of restorying when the child can try out new aspects of self by taking on a role and exploring a world in that role. A major aspect of this kind of play is the constant affirmation between child and therapist that it is 'only a story' so does not necessarily have to be lived in the reality world.

Claire and I sit together on the floor on our play mat. We have toys in small bags, which she can choose to use to play. I have a notebook in which to write her stories if that is the way she wants her play to be recorded. She selects her toys and begins to tell her story moving the toys about to show me what she means. She wants me to write down what she says. Claire tells this story to describe how abandoned she feels. She calls it Claire's Small Story. She was nine when she told it to me.

Claire's Small Story
There was once a river, a sort of nice place where people walked their dogs and sit on nice chairs.
Some people who were in love walked there because the river is heart shaped and it was lovely.
One day all the frogs ran out of the pool. Something made them run away and all that was left was the shape of the heart.
The lovers stayed in the chairs.
The lizards came and a few crocodiles came.
Soon the lovers saw some snakes moving in.
They were all slimy around, it looked all gooey.
The heart broke in pieces.
The snake put all the babies round his neck and killed them.

They gobbled the lovers up.
Everybody who loved each other died.

Claire had chosen small figures for her story and had made the river out of slime and play-doh. She knew from her parents the destructive power of love and experienced the loss of love from her parents. We recognised the hearts broken in the story and Claire felt powerful because she had been able to tell her story and stay with the sense of being heartbroken because it was only a story. The Arab storytellers start their stories with 'Kan-ma-kan,' which means, it was, it was not.

Narrative therapy

These processes of storying experiences are also explored in narrative therapy. Le Vay (2002) describes the expression of narrative identity as one of the fundamental processes in play therapy because this process enables the child and therapist to explore relationships via the symbolic and metaphoric imagery that is co-created during the course of the play.

Humans have a natural inclination to story personal experience and the richness of symbolism and metaphor in this process becomes embedded in the relationship between child and therapist. So narrative frameworks are constructed which allow children to begin to sequence, order, predict and make sense of complex feelings that can exist as a result of trauma and abuse.

Le Vay considers that we realise ourselves through the stories and narratives that we tell both ourselves and others. The words we say, the sentences we construct, and the events that we choose to include or omit all contribute to the generation of narrative identity through which we aim to make sense and order out of experience.

Lax (1992) states that the interaction itself is where the text exists and where the new narrative of one's life emerges. This unfolding text occurs between people, and in therapy clients unfold their stories in conjunction with a specific therapist so the therapist is always co-author of the unfolding story, with the client as the other co-author. The resulting text is neither the client's nor the therapist's story but a co-construction of the two.

Consider the story of the man with two wives. Each wife wants a different narrative about her husband.

When One Man Has Two Wives

A man had two wives and both loved him, though one was young and the other old.

Whenever the man lay down to sleep with his head on his young wife's knee, she would pull out the white hairs from his head so that he should look young like her.

And whenever he rested his head in his older wife's lap and slept she would pull out his black hairs so that he should be white haired like her.

And it was not long before the man was bald.

So the saying goes: Between Hannah and Bannah vanished are our beards.

Lax (1999) defines a narrative therapist as someone who assists persons to resolve problems by enabling them to deconstruct the meaning of the reality of their lives and relationships and to show the difference between the reality and the internalised stories of self. The narrative therapist encourages the client to re-author their own lives according to alternative and preferred stories of self-identity. Narrative therapy has links with those therapies that have a common respect for the client and an acknowledgment of the importance of context, interaction, bonding and the social construction of meaning.

Alan, aged six, has a story that we might explore together about why Superman put his mother in prison, what did she do and was it Superman's fault? We explore issues presented in the story which in some respects mirror Alan's feelings. It is safer to express those feelings as belonging to Superman's mum.

Once upon a time there was a boy called Superman.
He went to his cage and put his mum in prison.
She got very upset. She didn't like it there.
She cried and cried and cried and cried,
Until she calmed down.
The mum stays in prison
And Superman marries the girl.

I hear the story and value its importance because I respect Alan and his abilities to construct his identity through the stories he tells. There is equality in the relationship as we play with the story and expand our ideas about Superman and his mother, and what it feels like to be trapped or in prison. Only Alan has the answers to what happens in his story but I can ask questions.

The views of children are not often given value. It was interesting to hear of a research project by 'Save The Children' in Scotland (2002) when for the first time children had been asked what they thought about being smacked. The vast majority of children thought it was wrong and the older ones made a clear connection between being hit and adult violence. Amazing that no one had thought to ask the children before now!

Part of working with children's stories is to find other stories to tell so that there is a sense that human beings tell stories to each other. A Cree story called *The Stubbornness of Bluejays* describes a shift of identity through narrative. Noisy children enjoy it!

> *The Stubbornness of Bluejays*
> You know once there were some bluejays who lived in a tree and they were loud birds.
> Very loud always loud.
> There was a girl who often went to see them.
> Her name then was 'She who Tears-Things-Up'.
> Each time she saw the jays she asked them
> 'You jays you ever see me tear things up?'
> Well each time they heard this, those jays would begin arguing in the air.
> One would say, 'Yes, I saw you tear up a tree stump'.
> 'No I never did that' she would call back to the birds.
> 'Then how come you got that name?'
> One of the jays called to her with his screaming call.
> Then another bird screamed 'I saw you bite up a feather robe and spit it out.'
> Then the jay screamed its call at her.
> The girl said 'No I never did that.
> I hate you for saying that.
> Did you ever see feathers stuck in my teeth?'
> 'Just look' screamed the jay and each time the girl looked she found feathers in her teeth.
> 'These feathers weren't here when I arrived.
> One of you birds must have put them there.
> Who did it?'
> But all the jays chattered together until the whole tree in which they sat began to shake.

This made her angry because she knew they threw lies down at her from the tree.

She shouted back at them, 'I am going to argue louder than all of you.'

Then they all shrieked and shouted so loudly that when the girl spoke they couldn't hear her and it seemed that she was just moving her mouth.

And no words coming out.

After talking loud for such a long time she arrived home with a sore throat.

Her parents warned her and her sore throat warned her 'Don't go arguing with those jays.'

One morning she said to her parents
'I want a new name.'

Her father said 'Why is that?'

She said, 'Because I no longer tear things up, that is why.'
Then she said,
'I want the name "Able to Carry-On-Many-Arguments-At-Once."

It will help me against those jays.'

Again both her parents said 'Find another name.

That one will only get your throat in more trouble.'

Right away she went back and stood under the tree.

She argued at the jays.

She went on doing this.

There was a stubbornness which made her like one of those jays.

So she was given the new name.
'Who-Caught-Stubbornness-From-Jays.'

I enjoy that story and the way the girl reframes herself. No blame, you are who you are at certain moments in your life. Your parents try to protect as best they can and reach some sort of compromise where you can blame the blue jays for being argumentative!

The child as part of an ecological system

Bateson (1972) describes the person and the symbolic world of culture within a system of interdependent relations. He defined the unit of survival as a flexible organism-in-its-environment. He viewed the individual as part of a larger aggregate of interactional elements. These interactions involve information exchanges and it is the totality of these exchanges that makes up the mental process of the system in which the individual is only a part.

Bronfenbrenner (1979) defined the ecology of human development as progressive mutual accommodation between the growing human being and the changing properties of the immediate settings in which the developing person lives. This development is affected by relations between these settings and by the larger contexts in which the settings are embedded.

He defined three systems; the micro-(small) system, the meso-(middle) system and the exo-(large) system, all of which are contained in a *macro*-(large) system.

The micro-system is the child's life in the family with the daily routines, roles and interpersonal relations experienced by the developing person within the immediate setting of home and school.

The meso-system is the interrelations between two or more settings in which the developing child actively participates, for example, the relations between home, school and the local peer group. So a 'looked after' child may have a constantly changing system as they move from foster home to foster home that might also result in changes of school and peer group.

The exo-system refers to one or more systems that do not involve the developing person as an active participant but events occur in these systems that influence what happens in the setting containing the developing person. Thus, what happens in the parent's workplace, for example, could profoundly affect the environment of the child.

The macro-system is the culture and the society into which the individual is born. In this system are the cultural beliefs of the society, for example what it is like to be a child and how children should be reared.

Bronfenbrenner defines human development as a process through which the developing person acquires a more extended, differentiated and valid conception of the ecological environment, and becomes motivated and able to engage in activities that reveal the properties of, sustain or restructure that environment at levels of similar or greater complexity in form and content.

I have stated elsewhere (Cattanach 1997) that these ideas of ecological systems are important for the therapist who is considering whether a therapeutic intervention is appropriate and safe for the child who can be very powerless in their ecological environment. When the therapeutic hour is over, the child returns to that system and there must be some form of containment there for the child.

It is sometimes important for the therapist to explore aspects of the environment with the child and perhaps place some issues into a social context so the child has more understanding of their situation. Thus a child who is troubled by some of the behaviour of a parent who has bouts of mental illness might use dramatic play to describe their life together to make sense of the relationship. I might suggest that some information about the parent's illness would be helpful and that information sharing may also be part of the meetings because the child wants to understand and knowledge is power. That information sharing might also be part of a dramatic enactment or just straight talk. The child will decide.

Janet was 10. Her mother had bouts of severe depression and Janet wanted information about this illness and her mother's medication. She often used role-play to rehearse emergencies and how she would manage them. She role-played nurses and doctors at great length and all these activities helped her gain mastery over her family circumstances. Janet was a person living in a family and wanted to be able to cope with her particular circumstances in a practical way. Her story about herself and her family shifted when she had information about the nature of mental illness and ways of managing her mother's depression.

Jennings (1998) describes this beautifully when she states that successful therapy, in her view, places her in a context not only with other people but also in scenarios and landscapes that are significant in the world. She thinks that if she stays at the centre of her universe rather than being aware of others and thus part of a community, which means being socialised, she is unable to be aware of others unless she is able to be 'the other'.

Conclusions

> Continue to think and write even though reason is dead, history is over, the self is fractured, and knowledge is hopelessly enmeshed in oppressive relations of power.
>
> (Boyd 1999, no. 364)

When we start to work as therapists there is often a desire to find some deep truth, which will make us a miracle worker who can change the lives of children as if by magic. We seek the one truth of a particular method and negate all others, rather than incorporate the best of all ideas.

Consider this moral tale.

The Three Dervishes
Once upon a time there were three dervishes called Yak, Do and Se.

They came from the north, west and south respectively.

They had one thing in common.

They were looking for the Deep Truth and they sought a Way.

The first, Yak-Baba sat and thought until his head ached.

The second, Do-Agha stood on his head until his feet ached.

The third, Se-Kalandar, read books until his nose bled.

Finally they decided to work together.

They went into retirement and carried out their exercises together hoping that the energy from the three would produce the appearance of Truth, which they called the Deep Truth.

They persevered for forty days and forty nights.

At last in a whirl of smoke the head of a very old man appeared from the ground in front of them.

They asked him who he was.

Was he The Guide of Men, The Pillar of the Universe or The Changed One?

'I am none of these but I am that which you may think me to be.

Now you all want the same thing, which is the Deep Truth.'

'Yes O master' they replied.

'Have you heard the saying that there are as many Ways as there are hearts of men?' asked the head.

'In any case, here are your ways;

The First Dervish will travel through the Country of Fools,

'The Second Dervish will have to find the magic mirror and the third Dervish will have to call in the aid of the Jinn of the Whirlpool.'

So saying he disappeared.

The Dervishes talked about this among themselves.

They needed more information before setting out but also

because although they had all practised in different ways, each yet believed that there was only one way – his own – of course. Now none was certain that his own way was useful enough even though it had partly been responsible for summoning the apparition. Yak-Baba was the first to leave and whoever he met he asked if they knew the Country of Fools.

At last after many months he met someone who did know, and he set off there. As soon as he entered the country he saw a woman carrying a door on her back. 'Woman, why are you doing that?'

'Because this morning before my husband left for work he said, 'Wife there are valuables left in the house. Let nobody pass this door.' When I went out I took the door with me so that nobody could pass it. Now please let me pass you.'

'Do you want me to tell you something which will make it unecessary for you to carry the door?' asked Yak.

'Certainly not,' she said. 'The only thing that would help would be if you could tell me how to lighten the actual weight of the door.'

'That I cannot do,' said the Dervish so they parted.

Further on the Dervish met a group of people.

They were cowering in terror before a large watermelon, which had grown in a field.

'We have never seen one of these monsters before,' they told him 'and it will certainly grow much larger and kill us all. But we are afraid to touch it.'

'Would you like me to tell you something about it?' he asked them.

'Don't be a fool,' they replied. 'Kill it and you will be rewarded but we don't want to know anything about it.'

So the Dervish walked to the melon and cut a slice, which he started to eat.

Amid terrible cries of alarm the people gave him a handful of money.

As he left they said, 'Please don't come back, Honoured Murderer of Monsters.

Do not come and kill us likewise.'

Thus gradually in the Country of Fools in order to survive, he had to think and talk like a fool as well.

After several years he managed to convert some fools to reason and as a reward one day he attained Deep Knowledge.

But although he became a saint in the Country of Fools they remembered him only as the man who cut open the green monster and drank its blood.

They tried to do the same to gain Deep Knowledge but they never gained it.

Meanwhile Do-Agha the Second Dervish set off on his search for Deep Knowledge.

He just asked everyone he met if they had heard of the Magic Mirror.

Many misleading answers were given to him, but at last he realised where it might be.

It was suspended in a well by a piece of string as fine as a hair and it was itself only a fragment because it was made up of the thoughts of men, and there were not enough thoughts to make a whole mirror.

When he had outwitted the demon who guarded it, Do-Agha gazed into the mirror and asked for the Deep Knowledge.

Instantly it was his.

He settled down and taught in happiness for many years.

But because his disciples did not maintain the same degree of concentration needed to renew the mirror regularly it vanished away.

But to this day, there are many people who gaze into mirrors thinking that it is the magic mirror of Do-Agha the Dervish.

The Third Dervish Se-Kalandar looked everywhere for the Jinn of the Whirlpool.

The Jinn was known by many other names but Se-Kalandar did not know this and for years he always missed the Jinn because he was not known as Jinn of the Whirlpool in that place.

Finally after many years he came to a village and asked 'People, has anyone heard of the Jinn of the Whirlpool?'

'I have never hear of the Jinn' said a villager, 'but the village is called Whirlpool.'

Se-Kalandar threw himself on the ground and said, 'I will never leave this spot until the Jinn of the Whirlpool appears to me.'

The Jinn who was near-by swirled up to him and said 'We do not like strangers near our village, dervish. So I have come to you. What is it you seek?'

'I seek Deep Knowledge and I have been told that you can help me find it.'

'I can indeed,' said the Jinn. 'You have been through much.'
So the Jinn gave Se-Kalandar a programme of phrases, songs and actions to perform and phrases, songs and actions to avoid. 'Then you will gain Deep Knowledge.'
The Dervish thanked the Jinn and began his programme.
Months and years passed until he was able to perform his devotions and exercises correctly.
People came and watched him and began to copy him because of his zeal and because he was known to be a devout and worthy man. Eventually the Dervish attained Deep Knowledge, leaving behind him a devoted assembly of people who continued his ways.
They never did attain Deep Knowledge because they were beginning at the end of the Dervishes' course of study.
Afterwards when any of the adherents of these three Dervishes met, one says, 'I have my mirror here. Gaze enough and you will eventually gain Deep Knowledge.'
Another replies: 'Sacrifice a melon. It will help you as it did Yak-Baba.'
A third interrupts, 'Nonsense the only way is to persevere in the study and organizing of certain postures, of prayer and of good works.'
When they had in fact attained Deep Knowledge, the Three Dervishes found that they were powerless to help those whom they had left behind: as when a man carried away on a running tide may see a landlubber pursued by a leopard, and be unable to go to his help.

Chapter 4

Training and professional issues for play therapists

On becoming a play therapist. Learning and teaching

The Magpie's Nest
Once upon a time when pigs spoke rhyme
And monkeys chewed tobacco,
And hens took snuff to make them tough,
And ducks went quack, quack, quack, O!
All the birds of the air came to the magpie and asked her to teach them how to build nests. For the magpie is the cleverest bird of all in building nests.

So she put all the birds round her and began to show them how to do it. First of all she took some mud and made a round cake with it. 'Oh that's how it's done,' said the thrush; and away it flew, and so that's how thrushes built their nests.

Then the magpie took some twigs and arranged them round in the mud.

'Now I know all about it,' said the blackbird and off he flew; and that is how the blackbirds make their nest to this very day.

Then the magpie put another layer of mud over the twigs.

'Oh that's quite obvious,' said the wise owl, and away it flew; and owls have never made better nests since.

After that the magpie took some twigs and twined them round the outside.

'The very thing,' said the sparrow and off he went; so sparrows make rather slovenly nests to this day.

Well, then Madge Magpie took some feathers and stuff and lined the nest very comfortably with it.

'That suits me,' cried the starling, and off he flew; and very comfortable nests have starlings.

So it went on, every bird taking away some knowledge of how to build nests, but none of them waiting to the end.

Meanwhile Madge Magpie went on working without looking up till the only bird that remained was the turtle-dove, and that hadn't paid any attention all along, but only kept on saying it's silly cry, 'Take two, Taffy take two-o-o.'

At last the magpie heard this just as she was putting a twig across. So she said, 'One's enough.'

But the turtle-dove kept on saying 'Take two-o-o Taffy, take two-o-o.'

The magpie got really angry and said again 'One's enough.'

Still the turtle-dove cooed.

At last and at last the magpie looked up and saw nobody near her but the silly turtle-dove. She was really angry and flew away and refused to tell the birds how to build their nests again. And that is why different birds build their nests differently.

I think *The Magpie's Nest* describes how people use the learning process and also what it is like to teach. We take what we need from the learning situation, sometimes for better, sometimes, like the slovenly sparrows, for worse. There are misunderstandings between teacher and learners but everybody learns something which meets their particular needs. As a teacher myself I often felt like Madge Magpie and perhaps there is the same intensity in learning to build a nest for the young as there is in learning to be a therapist for the young.

Play therapy training

The learning programmes for play therapists are all postgraduate programmes and it is expected that candidates will have considerable experience of working with children. The criteria for entry to training is an appropriate professional qualification in teaching, psychology, paediatric occupational therapy, social work, etc., and/ or an appropriate first degree, for example an honours degree in psychology or a related subject.

Candidates for entry to the programmes must have substantial experience of working with children (no less than two years post-qualifying experience). Experience may be gained from health, social or educational services. Students are required to be working throughout the programmes.

All the recognised programmes are validated by a university or institute of higher education and approved by the British Association of Play Therapists. At present there are four recognised training programmes in York, London, Liverpool and Glasgow. The programmes vary in their theoretical perspectives but all focus on the centrality of play as the therapeutic process. It is important for all professionals who might be considering training as a play therapist to apply for a recognised training that is approved and has academic credibility.

The programmes are part-time and usually run over a two-year period. One university also runs a full-time programme that can be completed in just over one year. The length of this programme is determined by the time taken to complete placements, which usually take longer than an academic year. This programme is mainly for the benefit of overseas students who need to be in full-time study to gain a visa and live in the UK.

Some universities offer MA or MSc and PhD programmes, usually through a research dissertation. This has led to exciting research in subjects such as the content of the communication in play therapy sessions between child and therapist, interventions which can help children with specific difficulties, ideas about play and its meaning in the life of the child and narrative aspects of identity. Other MA programmes are completed after the Graduate Diploma through an extended piece of writing on a relevant topic of independent study.

All programmes include modules related to observations of children with their carers, play methods emphasising particular theoretical perspectives, theoretical and clinical issues related to children's problems and development, supervised practice and personal therapy. All aspects of the training are important. A therapist has to explore aspects of their own personal journey and their need to work with children through personal therapy, as well as knowledge and understanding of the theory and practice of play therapy.

The programmes have developed over the past ten years so it is still a new training with much exciting innovation. Key issues still to be resolved are the number of hours of supervised practice and the level of qualification required to practise as a play therapist. It is likely in future that the training will be longer; the qualification to practise will be at MA level with an extension to the number of hours of direct supervised practice with clients.

All the programmes are led by academics who are also practitioners of play therapy, so the vocational nature of the training is
clearly understood and a balance maintained between academic
disciplines and the practice of play therapy.

The British Association of Play Therapists (BAPT)

The Association of Play Therapists was formed in 1992 and added
British to its title in 1996 to avoid confusion with its American
counterpart.

The main aims are to promote and develop standards of practice
and training in play therapy, to encourage sharing of information,
experience and skills and to provide a national and regional
resource for its members.

Its objectives are as follows:

1. To stimulate an active interest in the development of play
   therapy.
2. To provide an understanding and awareness of play therapy.
3. To provide a support network for play therapists.
4. To provide information on relevant and specialised training
   courses.
5. To compile a directory of full and associate members.
6. To compile a list of members approved by the National
   Executive Committee of the BAPT to offer supervision.
7. To offer a forum of discussion of professional issues.
8. To distribute a regular journal/newsletter.
9. To organise an annual National Conference on issues relating
   to play therapy.
10. To hold an Annual General Meeting.
11. To maintain liaison with other professional groups involved in
    working with children.
12. To provide a Code of Ethics and Practice.
13. To do anything that may assist the attainment of the objectives
    of the British Association of Play Therapists.

Categories of membership are as follows:

1. *Full membership* is open to any person who holds a play
   therapy qualification recognised by BAPT, who is having

regular supervision, and is in or has recently had personal therapy.

2. *Associate membership* is open to any person training, working or interested in the field.

3. *Student membership*, which attracts a lower subscription rate than full or associate membership, is available to any person undertaking a training course validated by BAPT.

4. *Retired membership*, which attracts a lower subscription rate than full or associate membership, is available to any person who was a previous member of the association and has now retired from all paid employment, but has an interest in continuing to receive regular information about play therapy issues.

The Association has produced a Constitution, a Code of Ethics and Practice, a Complaints Procedure and an Equal Opportunities Policy.

The Constitution   The constitution is at present being updated and includes the philosophy of the Association, objectives and membership matters including membership entitlements and fees. The legal framework of the National Executive Committee is described with rules about officers, their length of service and such matters.

Code of Ethics and Practice   This is a crucial document for practising play therapists as it establishes and maintains standards for therapy and informs and protects members of the public using the services of play therapists who are members of BAPT.

The code of ethics defines core values of play therapy, client safety, therapeutic agreements and competence.

The code of practice defines issues of responsibility, client safety and client autonomy. It states that play therapy information given to members of the public should reflect accurately the training, qualifications and experience of the therapist and the service they offer.

The responsibility of the therapist for making clear the terms on which the therapy is being offered is described along with therapist competence and the responsibilities of therapists to themselves and to other play therapists. Play therapy supervision and consultative support are described as well as the extent of confidentiality that therapists are offering their clients.

The Code of Ethics and Practice is constantly updated to include new relevant criteria.

It is interesting to note that in March 2001, the Department of Health produced *12 key points on consent: the law in England*. Point 5 concerns children:

Can children consent for themselves?

5.   Before examining, treating or caring for a child, you must also seek consent. Young people aged 16 and 17 are presumed to have the competence to give consent for themselves. Younger children who understand fully what is involved in the proposed procedure can also give consent (although their parents will ideally be involved). In other cases, someone with parental responsibility must give consent on the child's behalf, unless they cannot be reached in an emergency. If a competent child consents to treatment, a parent **cannot** over-ride that consent. Legally, a parent can consent if a competent child refuses, but it is likely that taking such a serious step will be rare.

(Department of Health, 2001)

Supervision   The importance of supervision is stressed. All practising Full Members of the Association are required by the Code of Ethics and Practice to take all reasonable steps to monitor and develop their own competence and to work within the limits of that competence. This includes having appropriate and ongoing supervision with an approved supervisor.

In supervision the play therapist can discuss in confidence with the supervisor some of the feelings and issues brought up in the play therapy sessions. This helps to clarify what is happening for the child and can ensure that the child's needs are being met. Issues around appropriateness of referrals, planning and reviewing issues and the organisation of the therapy sessions can be discussed; however, supervision is not the same as line management or personal therapy but offers the opportunity for the therapist to develop professionally.

The Complaints Procedure   The aims of the procedure are to provide a means of considering any complaint about an infringement of the

BAPT Code of Ethics and Practice on the part of a Full Member of BAPT. The procedure is devised to protect both the complainant/client and the member. The procedure is continually revised to ensure the maintenance of high ethical standards.

Equal Opportunities Policy It is critical for an Association dealing with the lives of children to recognise that equal opportunities should be central within every aspect of policy and practice. BAPT is committed to promoting equal opportunities. The policy states:

> We acknowledge that institutional and individual oppression and discrimination exist and we are opposed to and committed to reducing them.
> We recognise that as a profession we are under-represented by people from a variety of cultural and racial backgrounds, by disabled people and by males and we would wish to address this through positive action.
> We would therefore actively encourage qualifying courses to accept applications from people from all under-represented groups.
> We expect that all courses will address core issues relating to race, gender and disability throughout their programme and this should be reflected in practice.

Play therapy as a profession

As play therapy has developed there is a move towards recognition as a profession. Lord Benson enunciated a definition of a profession in a speech in the House of Lords and this nine-point definition has now become the accepted one.

A Profession. Nine Obligations to the Public

1. The profession must be controlled by a governing body, which in professional matters directs the behaviour of its members. For their part the members have a responsibility to subordinate their selfish private interests in favour of support for the governing body.
2. The governing body must set adequate standards of education as a condition of entry and thereafter ensure that students obtain an acceptable standard of professional

competence. Training and education do not stop at qualification. They must continue throughout a member's professional life.

3.   The governing body must set the ethical rules and professional standards, which are to be observed by members. They should be higher than those established by the general law.

4.   The rules and standards enforced by the governing body should be designed for the benefit of the public and not for the private advantage of the members.

5.   The governing body must take disciplinary action, including if necessary expulsion from membership should the rules and standards it lays down not be observed, or should a member be guilty of bad professional work.

6.   Work is often reserved to a profession by statute, not because it is for the advantage of members, but for the protection of the public, it should only be carried out by persons with the requisite training, standards and discipline.

7.   The governing body must satisfy itself that there is fair and open competition in the practice of the profession so that the public are not at risk of being exploited. It follows that members in practice must give information to the public about their experience, competence, capacity to do the work and the fees payable.

8.   The members in the profession whether in practice or in employment, must be independent in thought and outlook. They must be willing to speak their minds without fear or favour. They must not allow themselves to be put under the control or dominance of any person or organisation, which could impair their independence.

9.   In the specific field of learning a profession must give leadership to the public it serves.

(Hansard Report of proceedings in the House of Lords. LD92/38 Job 6–11)

It would seem that through the development of training programmes in academic institutions, and the development and organisation produced by the British Association of Play Therapists over the past ten years, the work of the play therapist could now, according to the above criteria, be defined as a profession.

State registration

There is an increased demand for the services of play therapists in health, education and social services and it is important for the protection of the public to offer quality services which are regulated by the profession. There are a variety of approaches for strengthening and improving the quality of service provided. There is also an impetus from the government towards a modernised regulatory framework, with the emphasis on greater user and public representation, more transparent procedures and accountability.

The Health Act 1999 is committed to strengthening professional self-regulation, not only for those with a medical qualification but other staff as well. The National Institute for Clinical Excellence publishes guidelines concerning the evidence for treatment. The framework of clinical governance and approaches to strengthen lifelong learning all help support the work of those professions that support better mental health.

In an article in *Healthcare Counselling and Psychotherapy Journal* in 2001, Anne Richardson, Deputy Head, Mental Health Services Branch, Department of Health describes the issues, which professional bodies in counselling and psychotherapy need to address.

1. The issue of public protection. This needs to be addressed in two areas, firstly the abuse of clients and secondly within training the relationships between trainers and trainees.
2. The government approach is one of self-regulation. Professional bodies need to ensure that there is a clear consensus for, and understanding of, statutory regulation amongst the professionals themselves who would be affected.
3. Practitioners need to reach agreement on the criteria for delivering the main functions of a statutory register. This would include the content and process of training.
4. Details for the mechanisms of registration need to be considered. For example a category such as conditional registration is not a feature of the health professions council.
5. It is important to address the standards to be set for professional practice and continuing professional development. There could be a system for professional revalidation for those who do not make the grade, either at the point of

entry to the profession, or later, as a consequence of poor or
unprofessional practice.

(Richardson 2001, pp. 5, 6)

Richardson suggests that statutory regulation would bring significant benefits. There would be powers available to deal with
individuals who pose unacceptable risks to patients. There would
be directly elected practitioners and a strong lay input to carry the
responsibilities of setting and monitoring standards of professional
training, performance and conduct. There will be protection of
professional title linked to continuing professional development,
giving clearer professional identities for those who are qualified.

One way to support good practice might be to consider a model
for registration to be developed by the new Health Professions
Council that has replaced the Council for Professions Supplementary to Medicine.

The Council for Professions Supplementary to Medicine has
regulated twelve professions such as Speech Therapists, Physio-
therapists and Arts Therapists who have joined the Council at
various times since the Professions Supplementary to Medicine Act
1960.

In April 2001 the Department of Health published a document
called *Establishing the New Health Professions Council*. This new
Council replaces the Council for Professions Supplementary to
Medicine and its twelve boards that have regulated 120,000 prac-
titioners. The principal aims and objectives in setting up this new
Council were:

To reform ways of working by requiring the council to:
Treat the health and welfare of patients as paramount
Collaborate with and consult key stakeholders
Be open and pro-active in accounting to the public and
professions for its work.

To reform structures and functions by:
Giving wider powers to deal effectively with individuals who
pose unacceptable risks to patients
Creating a smaller council comprising directly elected practitioners and a strong lay input, charged with strategic
responsibility for setting and monitoring standards of professional training, performance and conduct

Linking registration with evidence of continuing professional development

Providing stronger protection of professional roles

Enabling the extension of regulation to new groups.

(Department of Health, 2001)

If play therapists were to choose state registration the development of this new Council could be the way forward. There would then in the future be a statutory register of play therapists. The main functions of such a register would be selection for entry to the profession, training, continuing professional development, registration, fitness to practise and discipline.

State registration would define a universal standard, which would be in the public domain through the register and the title State Registered Play Therapist would be protected to indicate that its holder has achieved educational and clinical standards and is governed by a disciplinary and ethical code.

There are disadvantages in that play therapists would have to join with other similar professions to form a large enough group to be represented at the Council and that group would be just one body within a much larger number of professions. It could be difficult to emphasise the uniqueness of the discipline in such a large body as the Health Professions Council. This no doubt is a matter to be addressed when the Council sets up its organisational structures.

Representatives on such Councils are often heavily weighted towards academics, who seem to be the only professionals with time and money to attend meetings. Their clinical expertise is often very limited with minimum clinical work experience in the public sector so the regulations they make are often not viable in clinical situations, although their expertise is required on training matters. There needs to be a balance of clinical and academic expertise. This also may be addressed by the new Council.

The functions of the British Association of Play Therapists would be considerably changed if the profession becomes a registrant of the Health Professions Council, which has a training brief to validate and approve courses. At present this is a function of the Association.

Continuing professional development (CPD)

With the impetus for a modernised regulatory framework for health professionals comes the requirement for lifelong learning.

This is considered to be an essential requirement for all practitioners in a modern health and social care environment. It therefore requires both a personal and a corporate commitment. Every professional should have a personal development plan, which would be reviewed annually, and local learning plans should be supported by protected time for learning activities.

The learning plan should contribute to the maintenance of professional competence and the development of new skills, which support and extend academic knowledge and provide opportunities for personal reflection on practice as a play therapist. Part of this learning should also be multi-professional to support effective team working and perhaps this could be started as part of the initial training or a post-qualifying project.

BAPT has set up a working party to explore CPD and the group has presented a proposal for discussion. The group examined the criteria of other professional organisations and no doubt the Health Professions Council will suggest its own criteria in due time.

The BAPT proposal for discussion suggests the following:

CPD – an average of 24 hours per year over a 3-year period, with no less than 12 hours in any one year; increasing to an average of 36 hours per year in two stages over 2/3 years) of which:

Supervision   33% minimum
                 50% for qualified practitioners with less than 2/3 years' experience
Training events 33% minimum: all hours to be face-to-face contact and not to include breaks

Any remaining hours to be made up from a list of agreed activities such as:

Providing clinical supervision, or training/teaching to others
Attendance at BAPT accredited courses
Attendance at courses which members think relevant to their practice
Research on play therapy
Attendance on a post-qualifying course for play therapy.

(A variety of other options are listed and a form for logging hours has been devised.)

Conclusions

Over the past 15 years in the UK, play therapy has emerged as an effective way of helping children and young people who are experiencing distress. Training programmes are now offered in universities and institutes of higher education. BAPT is now 10 years old and members have worked hard to establish criteria to develop play therapy as a profession. This has meant that standards of practice have risen and safeguards have been put in place to protect the vulnerable children we serve and support. One issue to be considered is salary scales for play therapists and perhaps BAPT should consider some alliance with a supportive union, which has skills in salary negotiations.

It is to be hoped that registration will be effective and rules and regulations made for the benefit of clients and practitioners rather than professional administrators. The creativity of the play therapist should not be strangled in meaningless administrative tasks, which do nothing to protect the client or therapist. The professional development of the therapist, as part of lifelong learning, should be supported by the organisation in which the therapist works by protected time and financial remuneration.

Professional matters can become all consuming so remember this story.

The Dogs Hold an Election
The Brule Sioux have a story about elections.
Once a long time ago, the dogs were trying to elect a president.
So one of them got up in the big dog convention and said,
'I nominate the bulldog for president. He is strong he can fight.'
'But he can't run,' said another dog.
'What good is a fighter who can't run?
He won't catch anybody.'
Then another dog got up and said,
'I nominate the greyhound, because he sure can run.'
But the other dogs cried: 'Now he can run alright,
But he can't fight.
When he catches up with someone, what then?
He gets the hell beaten out of him, that's what!
So all he's good for is running away.'
Then an ugly little mutt jumped up and said:

'I nominate that dog for president who smells good underneath his tail.'

And immediately an equally ugly mutt jumped up and yelled: 'I second that motion.'

At once all the dogs started sniffing underneath each other's tails.

A big chorus went up.

'Phew he doesn't smell good underneath his tail.'

'No, neither does this one.'

'He's not president timber.'

'No, he's no good either.'

'That one sure isn't the people's choice.'

'Wow, this ain't my candidate.'

When you go out for a walk.

Just watch the dogs.

They're still sniffing underneath.

They're looking for a good leader.

And they still haven't found him.

But above all we must not forget the fragility of the relationship between child and therapist and what rests at the core of that relationship.

Butterflies. A Papago legend

One day the Creator was resting, watching some children at play in a village.

The children laughed and sang; yet as he watched them, the Creator's heart was sad.

He was thinking: 'These children will grow old.

Their skin will become wrinkled.

Their hair will turn grey.

Their teeth will fall out.

The young hunter's arm will fail.

The playful puppies will become blind, mangy dogs.

And those wonderful flowers, yellow and blue, red and purple will fade.

The leaves from the trees will fall and dry up.

Already they are turning yellow.'

Thus the Creator grew sadder and sadder.

It was in the autumn
And the thoughts of the coming winter,
With the cold and loss of green leaves
Made his heart sad.
Yet it was still warm
And the sun was shining.
The Creator watched the sunlight and the shadow,
He saw the beautiful colours of the flowers
And the way the wind blew the leaves round and round
He saw the blue sky and the white cornmeal.
Then he smiled and said,
'I must make something to preserve all these colours.
Something for the children to look at which will make their
hearts happy.'
So the Creator took out his bag and started gathering things.
He gathered a spot of sunlight, a corner of the blue sky,
The whiteness of cornmeal,
The red, purple, orange and white of the flowers,
The green of the pine needles,
He put them all in his bag and
The last thing he took was the songs of the birds.
Then he walked over to the grass where the children were
playing.
'Children, little children, this is for you.'
And he gave them his bag.
'Open it there is something nice inside for you.'
The children opened the bag and at once hundreds and
hundreds of coloured butterflies flew out,
Dancing about the children's heads,
Settling on their hair, fluttering up and down
to sip nectar from the flowers.
And the children said that they had never seen anything so
beautiful.
The butterflies began to sing
and the children listened enchanted.
But then a songbird came flying
Settling on the Creator's shoulder scolding him saying,
'It's not right to give our songs to these new pretty things.
You told us when you made us that every bird would have its
own song.
And now you've passed them all around.

Isn't it enough that you give your new playthings the colours of the rainbow.'
'You're right,' said the Creator,
'I made one song for each bird, and I shouldn't have taken what belongs to you.'
So the Creator took the songs away from the butterflies
And that's why they are silent.
'They're beautiful, even so,' he said.

Chapter 5

Settings for play therapy

Louis XIII's Amusements 1601–1608
The list of toys given to Louis XIII, the future king of France

In 1601: a hobby-horse, a windmill, a whipping top, a tambourine, soldiers, a cannon, a tennis-racket, a ball, clockwork pigeon, scissors, cutting paper, and dolls (male only). At four, the future king was practising archery, playing cards, playing racket ball, and joining in such parlour games as fiddle-de-dee, hand clapping and hide and seek. At six he played chess, trades, charades and pantomime. At seven – the transitional age when he would no longer be educated by women – he was forbidden to play with dolls and soldiers, and the skills of riding, hunting, fencing, shooting and gambling replaced his toys. He continued, however, to play such games as blindman's bluff, I-sit-down, and hide and seek, since they, too, were part of the adult world.

(The Penguin Book of Childhood)

Introduction

Play therapy is not yet a recognised profession with its own pay scales and employment conditions but it is valued as a way of working with children in many areas of their lives. The training for play therapists is post-qualifying so the therapist will also have qualifications such as a social worker, teacher, occupational therapist, psychologist, clinical nurse and the like. This often means that play therapy is part of their work but not the whole.

Play therapy can be used in a variety of settings both in the public sector and in private practice. The main settings for play therapy in the public sector are in health, social services and education. The main role of play therapists in both public and private practice is to offer therapy to children, to help support families who have struggles with their children, to train other professionals about the use of play and the function of play therapy with children, to train the carers of children about aspects of play and child care issues and to make assessments about the needs of children.

It is important for the work in these settings to be undertaken by qualified play therapists. As has been stated, the play therapist sometimes has other roles within the organisation for which they work. In those circumstances the roles must be clear and not overlap each other. For example, a social worker who is also a qualified play therapist cannot make decisions about whether a child should be taken into care in the role of the social worker and offer play therapy to that child about their family circumstances at the same time. This would be a breach of the child's right to confidentiality. And the therapeutic relationship would be distorted by the social work role of the therapist. But children who are in the care of other social workers could be referred for play therapy because the roles of social worker and play therapist would not then conflict with each other.

Play can be used as a way of making an assessment of the child's needs if it is made clear that assessment is the function of the intervention. This is a different process from play therapy to help the child make sense of troubling experiences, although assessment done sensitively can help children understand what has happened to them and their family and is in that sense therapeutic. In using play for assessment purposes the child must be very clear about the levels of confidentiality within that relationship as well as the function of an assessment and what it might mean for the child's future.

The teaching role of the play therapist is an important way to help other professionals understand what play therapy is about and how to use play within other professional areas. It is helpful to show carers in whatever settings they meet with children how to use play to help with communication and as a way to enhance attachment between child and adult. Many professionals still think that play therapy is a precursor to talking therapies and it is helpful to show that it is a discrete discipline with theoretical concepts emerging from practice.

Play therapy in the health service

Child and Adolescent Mental Health Services

The most common setting for play therapy in the health service is in child and family support known as Child and Adolescent Mental Health Services (CAMHS). These services offer specialist, multi-disciplinary diagnostic assessment, treatment, advisory and consultative services for children and adolescents where there are mental health needs. These needs are defined as psychiatric disorders, or where behaviour, emotional state or development is causing serious concern to themselves or those caring for them.

These services are often divided into primary care and specialist care teams. The primary care teams cover child and family mental heath needs and support the work of GPs, health visitors and other professionals working in the community. The specialist teams cover very specific issues like eating disorders or complex child abuse matters. The use of specialist teams is determined by the referrals made to that particular service. The team in CAMHS is multi-disciplinary from health, education and social services and this offers a broad perspective of ideas and understanding that is very helpful in considering the needs of families who come to the service. It also means that a variety of therapeutic interventions can be offered to individuals and families. Referrals to the service can be self-referral, from GPs, health visitors, school health, educational psychologists, social services and other such sources.

Play therapists are a valuable resource for both primary and specialist care and have a place in all the services offered. There is sometimes a tendency to think that play therapists only work with young children or those with language difficulties so it is important for the play therapist to be able to explain how important play can be to all clients who come for help with mental health issues. Sometimes parents are unable to play with their children or do not recognise the value of play as a means of communication so there is a useful role for the play therapist in helping adults in their dealings with children.

The multi-disciplinary approach creates a high-quality service shared between a variety of professionals. Joint working by professionals can give a child and family maximum support to meet a range of issues created by family difficulties. An example of such joint working might be helping a mother and daughter where the child had been sexually abused. The mother could receive help and support from a professional in the service while the child has play therapy. The pattern of such an intervention might be that professionals and family meet together at the beginning of the session, then child and parent separate for individual help, and then all meet at the end to reflect together and plan for future meetings.

Working together in CAMHS

An example of such an approach is the assessment and support for children with Attention Deficit Hyperactivity Disorder (ADHD). I ran a group for such children which is described in Chapter 6. Assessments for ADHD were offered at the clinic once every three months. The staff team conducting the assessments included child psychiatrists and their registrars, clinical psychologists, a child psychiatric nurse, paediatricians and a play therapist.

During assessments I worked with the child psychiatric nurse and we devised a programme of play for a group of children to observe their behaviour. While we played with the children, other professionals interviewed the families. When we had finished the play we took the children back to their family to complete the family assessment.

When that was completed the professionals met together to discuss their findings and suggest recommendations for the family that were then taken back to the family for their consideration.

Families whose child was assessed with ADHD were offered a variety of options including parenting groups for the adults, support for the child and possibly medication depending on the circumstances.

As a play therapist, I offered to run a group to support the children who had been diagnosed with ADHD. This was valued by the children who enjoyed the opportunity to play in a group and negotiate their relationships with each other. This also gave me insight about how each individual child managed peer relationships. Having learnt from the interactions in the group I was able to offer further suggestions about caring for these children to parents and carers and the professionals in the service who were offering long-term support to parents.

Paediatric services

Play therapy can assist the care and support for children in hospital. Support for children who have chronic illness could be offered in such circumstances although this might be offered by CAMHS or the hospital psychology service. Some children, however, reject talking about their circumstances, and prefer to use play as a way to describe their feelings about being in hospital. They find symbolic play a safe way to express their situation.

Sometimes there is confusion about the role of the play therapist and the hospital play specialist whose role is to help the child manage the practicalities of the treatment process and explain procedures and treatment to the child.

Play therapists can support children with life threatening illnesses through work in hospices and hospitals. Some therapists offer support for children who aren't sure if they want to continue treatment. Maureen Scott Nash narrates such an intervention in a chapter in *The Story So Far* (2002), which describes the struggles of a boy coping with leukaemia. He used a variety of symbols and stories to describe his fight with the illness and the strategies he used to cope with the treatment. Scott Nash states that the very nature of this illness makes the child vulnerable to a sense of loss of control. Bodily processes that were always taken for granted are suddenly in question as the administration of the treatment can seem to overtake the very being of the child and feelings of helplessness prevail. In play therapy Jamie found a way to play out his deep sense of anger at the repeated assaults on his body as he recovered from the procedures imposed on his body.

Alison Webster, who is a Team Manager for Play Specialists and is herself a play therapist, has devised a brief intervention for young people who have repeated admissions to hospital to help them express the frustrations they feel about the disruption hospital brings to their lives. It is described more fully in Chapter 8. One of the issues for the play therapist in a hospital setting is to manage an intervention within the organisation of a big hospital so the child doesn't feel overwhelmed by professionals, leading to further confusion and anxiety. The meetings have to be in the time frame of repeated hospital visits so short-term interventions are more appropriate in this setting.

Children often find it difficult to express how they feel about their treatment in hospital and doctors also find it difficult to think that children experience them as monsters who hurt them as well as kind people who might cure them. Some children need a safe place to express this duality without feeling that they are letting down their family or the medical staff.

Social services

Play therapists can have a key role in supporting children who are involved with social services for a variety of reasons.

Assessments

Play therapy processes can be used as part of the assessment procedure so long as the child is aware that this is what is happening. This kind of assessment is often requested from a legal instruction for a court hearing. Requests for such assessments may come from social services or the courts and are sometimes undertaken on an independent basis by a play therapist who is recognised as an expert witness for court proceedings. This assessment can be a therapeutic experience for the child and family but it is vital that the child is aware of the function of the assessment and how the information they give will be used. This knowledge about the meaning of the meetings between child and therapist should be given to the child on a regular basis during the assessment so that when a report is written the child doesn't feel betrayed. Children have the right not to disclose information about their family if they do not wish to do so. Many children will not say very much during an assessment because they do not want to betray their family.

Kate Kirk is an experienced play therapist with an expertise in making family assessments. Here she writes about this process.

My Court work is usually focused on assessment of attachments and child/parent interaction. I work in a very structured way, which suits my temperament. I use a mixture of non-directive play and structured techniques.

I tend to outline the play assessment methodology at the beginning of my report as this makes life easier for me if I am cross-examined later in the process. The work process should be like a story with a beginning, a middle and an end. Doing this makes it easier for the lawyers and the judge to see how and why I reached a particular conclusion.

The play assessment methodology

The parents

I usually explain to the parents both verbally and in a written letter via their solicitor that I will use a play therapy assessment tool called the Marschak Interaction Method (MIM) (Marschak et al. 1993) in order to observe the parents' ability to:

- use play purposefully with the child
- behave playfully with the child/ren
- alert the child/ren to the environment
- give affection to the child/ren and reduce stress.

In this part of the assessment participant observation is the principal method used. The first family session would be a general observation session of an hour and a half. The parent/s can do whatever they want in that time and my play equipment is made available to them. The second session is structured into the four tasks mentioned above.

I generally use a video recorder for the family sessions, as it is useful when there are several experts involved and it is useful too in supervision providing that appropriate consent has been given in writing.

The aim underpinning this method of assessment is to observe how a parent and child respond to each other. It also enables me to gain additional information from a historical perspective on how the child is parented and whether or not they allow their stress to be reduced by the parents or carers.

I would also use the CARE Index (Belsky et al. 1997) as the theory underpinning my ideas on care giving and it aids the MIM. It enables me to assess the parents'/carers' ability to provide for the children's basic need for food, warmth and shelter as well as providing stability, age-appropriate boundaries and continuity of care.

As social-developers of their children I would look at their ability to be a playmate and a teacher shaping and developing their children's world. As attachment figures their primary role is to provide security within the relationship and protect the child from harm, encouraging safe exploration of the environment to develop age-appropriate autonomy.

Within the MIM there is a measure called the Leave the Room Test that for a younger children can also provide information on how the children cope with separation from the parent and reunion. However, in assessment of attachment it is never wise to rely just on one measure and I also use the following measures to gather data from the adults on the children's relationship as well as an outline of their overall functioning within their current family situation:

- Questionnaires for foster carers and teachers.
- Semi-structured interviews for other relatives who know the child.
- Sibling relationship checklists for people who know the child well.

The child

In my assessment work with the child I usually ask why they think they have come to my room. I explain what I have been asked to do in child-friendly language. I use four non-directive play sessions to evaluate the play behaviour. I verbalise the actions and reflect the feeling states, looking out for connecting themes in the sessions.

I also have two structured sessions using projective expressive techniques:

- The Draw A Person Inquiry (DAPI Robinson 1997) to ascertain the child's ability to recognise feeling states.
- For an older child I would usually follow this exercise with a Colour Metaphor, which strengthens information obtained from the DAPI and the play behaviour. This method matches colours to feelings and explores how much of the child's life has been filled with the feelings described by the colours selected. It is called The Colour Your Life Technique by O'Connor and described in the *Handbook of Play Therapy* (O'Connor 1983).

I would usually end with the Make a Sand Game: this is an Island Game in the sand, used as a further projective method of assessing the child's attachments, who meets their basic needs for food, warmth and shelter and their higher emotional needs for stimulation and fun. Looking at whom the child places on the island and who is left off will be informing the process.

I might also use story completion tests as a means of assessing the children's view of their parenting figures as this sets the tone for all their other relationships. Story completion tests have been widely researched as a means of finding out what mental representations of family life children are left with when they have experienced severe abuse and neglect.

I find that by using a combination of non-directive and structured methods I can usually get sufficient information on the child's perspective at that time to give the court a view. Similarly, observation of the parent/child interaction portrays the positive and negative aspects of the relationships at that time.

Kate works on family assessments as well as with the child and this thorough method is helpful when decisions have to be made about the needs of children within a family situation. She makes it clear to all family members that it is an assessment but uses material that is based on play therapy methods that have been validated and are based on empirical data.

Play therapists are asked to make assessments of a variety of family issues; such questions as contact between child and birth family when the child is separated, sibling contact and the difficulties children might experience living with a parent with mental health problems, are examples of requests for assessment. It is important that the therapist has a list of questions from the solicitor, which delineate what information the court is seeking. This means that the therapist has specific objectives and this can help the communication between child and therapist.

This is a task for an experienced play therapist who has considerable knowledge of local authority systems in social work and legal knowledge in matters relating to children and families as well as extensive experience of play therapy.

Play therapy after assessment

Once assessments of child and family are complete, decisions will be made about the need for therapy for child and family members. This is usually decided in formal meetings of professionals, when future planning for the family is determined.

Sometimes assumptions are made about therapeutic needs that are not based on the individual person within their environment but on what has happened to them. For example, not all abused children will need a therapist to support them after abuse and sometimes it is better to work with the child's carers to help them support the child. One of the difficulties for children looked after in the care system is the number of professionals they see in the course of the assessment process and thereafter. It can become difficult for the child to form attachments to parent figures and to discriminate between adults and their purpose in the life of the child. It is not helpful for the child to perceive the therapist as the parent if new adoptive parents are trying to fulfil that role for the child.

Therapy after abuse

Many children will find play therapy a helpful way to explore their feelings in relation to abuse they experienced if that is the reason for coming into care. The child must be in a safe enough place to be able to reflect on what has happened. If abuse has meant the loss of family, then this also has to be explored. Children who take responsibility for their abuse and the loss of family find it very difficult to discard their sense of victimisation. The symbolic nature of play therapy can help to ease the pain because all the feelings associated with the abuse can be expressed in the safety of play.

It is important that the therapist is not used by the child protection team to find out what is going on in a family under the guise of therapy. Therapy should be part of treatment and not part of the investigation, which is a matter for social services child protection teams. The reason for an intervention must be very clear to both child and therapist, with an understanding about what information remains confidential and what has to be reported as a matter of child protection. The assessment process should be complete before therapy begins.

If a child is not in care but living in a difficult family situation, then work must be done with all family members, so that the therapist is not perceived as a rescuer by the child or as a person colluding with abuse. It is not helpful to the child if therapy has been forced on the family against the wishes of the parents. Often agreements can be mediated with the parents but if this does not happen then the therapy will be undermined by the carers. This can also happen with children in foster care and work must be done with carers so that they do not undermine the child and/or therapist. If the adult carers are not supportive, the child can be left with the idea that they do not deserve to be nurtured and nothing nice can happen without some degree of punishment.

Janice told this story about the family.

The Family
There is a mum and a dad.
The dad goes to work

And the mum works at home.
They were horrible.
They were shouting to the children
When the kids were naughty.
And when the kids weren't doing anything.
Both mum and dad hit the children.
They were not rude.
The children didn't leave
But stayed to be scared.
The mum and dad were always horrible.
They never did anything nice for the children
In all their lives.
The End.

An initial meeting with the child and carers should explore the reasons for the intervention and some of the issues that are troubling the child so that a formulation of the needs of the child can be discussed with both child and carers. If the adults need support it should be offered at the same time as therapy for the child so that the adults have their own place to get support. If this does not happen the adult carers will often try to use the play therapist to support their needs to the detriment of the relationship between child and play therapist.

It is often helpful for the play therapist and child to share some aspects of their relationship with carers. What is shared will be negotiated between child and therapist but if this is done at the end of the session, the child feels held by both therapist and carers who in their turn do not feel excluded. The child lives with their carers and therapy shouldn't split that relationship, but the child's right to confidentiality should also be respected.

Children sometimes want to offer a drawing they have done in therapy to their carers. I suggest that the drawings done in therapy are private but a special drawing for the carer can be made and given at the end of the session. Drawings and objects made in therapy are an expression of the emotional life of the child and should remain confidential to the intervention and not used as though they are recreational material.

Sometimes it is more helpful for the play therapist to support the parents of a child who has difficulties so that the parents become therapists. For example, I worked with parents whose child had been sexually abused by a neighbour. The child had disclosed to her mother who had coped well and appropriately reported the matter to the police and social services.

The parents felt they could cope with helping their child themselves. They also felt that they, the adults, were experiencing more distress and wanted a space to express how they felt. But they also wanted to find ways of helping their daughter. Initially they expressed the rage and anguish they felt. They experienced this in different ways and were antagonistic to each other but always ended up supporting each other. We shared ways of listening to distasteful details of the abuse without showing disgust when their daughter talked to them. They didn't want her to feel that they were disgusted with her. We explored the helplessness they felt and the fact that they hadn't realised what was going on with their neighbour who they had considered a loving grandfather figure for their child. There were arguments between mother and father about ways to proceed but these were resolved. Tension came when the matter went to court. They all coped well with the situations as they arose and they were able to support each other through each distressing event. There was a feeling of resolution when the court case ended with a term of imprisonment for the perpetrator but the lives of the family had been changed irrevocably. They survived together as a family and the parents were most capable therapists/ parents in dealing with their daughter's experience. They felt that the help they had received was a support throughout the proceedings to the end of the court case and they thought it most important they had helped their daughter but with guidance and help from the therapist. Their daughter also wrote to thank me, although we had never met she knew that her parents met me and were helped which then supported her.

Helping children move to adoption

This is an important process for children who are being looked after by the local authority and are in foster or residential care waiting for a new family. In this transitional state it has been considered in the past that therapy was not appropriate. However, Ruth Watson (2002) has explored this transitional stage as a rite of passage and suggests that in play therapy the child can define rituals and play to express the stages of loss and grief they experience before moving towards a new attachment with a new family. The therapy continues in the adoptive family if at all possible so the child feels contained by the therapist until settled with the new family. Watson describes the rituals established between a child and therapist to express the shift from one life to another and how these symbols and rituals were repeated in an effort to express and share endings and new beginnings. She describes how the use of 'love hearts' to express different forms of love and hate became one symbol and part of the rituals expressed in the process of discovering meaning in finding a family.

Sometimes children have a long wait for a new family and it can be helpful to express this during the waiting time. These are the issues explored in therapy as well as the here and now of everyday experience as they wait to move on. Some children choose to live very much in the present if the past was intolerable and the future is unknown. The therapist must follow the desires of the child and the choices they have made as they try their best to cope with the uncertainty of not knowing who is to care for them in the long term. Stories at this time are often about abandonment. This is what Rachel played.

> The little girl lives with mummy and daddy.
> The dog is naughty.
> He goes in the dustbin but he is really nice.
> The little girl with broken legs lives nowhere.
> Her mummy and daddy are not there.
> She goes on a bike.
> She is sad.
> Another mum gives her clothes.
> Her mum and dad didn't do anything.
> She is just sad.
> She is going to another home to live.
> She is pleased.
> The little girl is so tired she goes to bed at bedtime.
> The daddy is little.
> The snake comes along.
> Mummy goes on the snake and goes round and round.
> The End.

After adoption

Some children experience distress after adoption and will require help to cope with the loss of their birth family and adjustment to a totally new way of life. These difficulties can emerge any time and for some children there seems to be a cycle of peaceful times and then anxious moments. I have worked with some children on and off during childhood, as usually with these situations the children know to ask for support when they need to make sense of some issues which are troubling them. Some children need to express their yearning for their birth family, their old friends, pets, streets, the man at the fish and chip shop, even though they want to stay with their adoptive family. They don't want to hurt their new family so don't talk about the past or don't know how to tell people what they want and need because they don't feel they deserve that kind of respect. Sometimes the therapist can help to mediate the new relationships and encourage the new attachments.

Stories told by children often express ideas about good places and scary places. Often good places turn into scary places and children in adoptive families are anxious that this will happen in their new family. This was Amy's story. She wasn't sure she could trust her new family to be different and care for her. She made the lake with 'slime' and placed the toys in the lake.

The Lake
This is a nice lake.
It has no name.
It is full of creatures.
The water is warm and nice.
The creatures just float all day.
There are so many they get on top of each other.
They begin to fight.
They just fight and fight.
Some creatures get killed.
Lots of bruises, no blood.
The creatures cry and scream.
Some creatures die and they are buried.
The lake which was once warm and nice
Is now full of terror.
The creatures are so scared
They can hardly breathe.
There are some children, some grown-ups.
Some children get killed by the fighting.
Blood comes out of them and they die.
It is the parents that kill them

Because the parents got angry.
The big monster goes in the lake and scares everybody.
It's a woman monster with big eyes.
And she eats creatures and swallows them.
The End.

If there are difficulties in attaching to the new family it may be helpful to offer indirect help via parent co-therapy. Hart and Thomas (2000) describe this process in an article entitled, 'Controversial attachments. The indirect treatment of fostered and adopted children via parent co-therapy'. Only the parent/carer deals directly with the child. The lead therapist and parent collaborate to reduce the exposure of the child to other professionals. The work between lead and co-therapist is conducted within a therapeutic space and the lead therapist sets the boundaries. The lead therapist becomes an attachment figure for the parents, offering a long-term commitment to provide a secure space to explore the child's worlds. This is an interesting way to help fostered and adopted children make new attachments and could be adapted for use by play therapists.

Play therapy in schools

Play therapy can be used in many ways in schools to support children who are experiencing difficulties in that environment. Group or individual therapy can be helpful for children who find school a difficult place to be. Preparatory work is essential so that any intervention is supported by staff in the school and the carers of the children. Sometimes teachers think that therapy will help them find out what is happening in the child's life. It is important to offer school staff information about play therapy and the confidential nature of the relationship in therapy. It is important to know if other professionals outside the school system are involved with the child and family, otherwise there can be professional overload and the child feels stigmatised by yet another adult.

Helpful work can be undertaken at school with children who have special needs. The work for the play therapist can be around issues that emerge for children and adolescents at particular life stages. Sometimes it can be to assist a teacher and the child's key worker to explain a life event to the child who could have difficulty with verbal communication. In this process it is often important to find an interest of the child and use this as a way to explain what needs to be told. For example, I worked with the key worker and a 12-year-old girl who had very limited language to give information about the fact that Mary, the 12-year-old, was to go into foster care because her mother was unable to continue to look after her. Mary had a great interest in cars and passengers in cars so we were able to use drawing cars as a way to introduce the subject of her move to a new family. We used drawing, placing toys and objects in the room to delineate present home and new home, photographs of family and foster family and all our acting talents to play out the move to the new family. As the play therapist I worked with the key worker, instigated the play, which was then endlessly repeated at the request of Mary until she developed some understanding of what was to happen. When she met the foster family she had seen their photographs many times and her move to the new family was to some extent less surprising than if she had not had the repeated play.

Children with a variety of learning disabilities want to play and describe what has happened to them, perhaps in a very simple form. John was in a special school and struggled with his attention difficulties and anxiety about the physical abuse he had been subjected to in the past. He made simple stories, which described this and his yearning for a life without violence.

> *The Snake Family*
> The snakes are a family, mum, dad and a girl.
> Her name is Ce Ce.
> They get on well.
> No shouting, no hitting.
> But they do a little bit of hitting.
> The snakes like it
> But John and Ann, they don't like being hit.

Jane was nearly sixteen and was anxious about taking responsibility and what it means to leave school and be grown up. She has a genetic disorder with learning difficulties. She called this Jane's Story.

> *Jane's Story*
> Once upon a time my dad and me lived together in a big house with mum.
> Sometimes Jane was bad, sometimes Jane was good,

But most of the time Jane was angry and stamped around and hit herself.

Mum and dad said,

'You naughty girl, in your room now.'

Jane said she was sorry and she wouldn't ever do it again.

Jane apologised.

Dad said he loved her so no more arguing.

This is all over because Jane is nearly grown up,

And grown-ups can't argue.

Jane is so big she will soon be going to work.

After college Jane is going to the hostel to sleep.

Jane isn't angry anymore with the lady who hit her at the hostel.

There is no more shouting.

Jane is a bit scared of shouting.

The End.

Both John and Jane feel vulnerable about themselves and fearful about the future and what they might be expected to do. Jane was worried about going to college and how she would cope with a gradual separation from her parents. They enjoyed the individual attention from the therapist and developed an awareness of themselves and how to manage some of their fears. The emotions of children with special needs are often brushed aside and it is very important that there is time and a safe space to express how they feel.

Project work in schools

Many teachers are concerned that children are taught very little about emotional intelligence or emotional literacy. Emotional intelligence can be defined as knowing one's emotions, managing emotions, motivating oneself, recognising emotions in others and handling relationships. Emotional literacy is described as the ability to understand one's own emotions and those of other people and to handle and express these emotions in a productive way.

Play therapists can support projects to develop emotional literacy in schools. The Hopes Project was one such idea.

The Hopes Project

This project was initiated in some schools in Harrow in 2000 by a group of professionals from health, social services and education together with a young person representative of Young People with Voices (which is young people in contact with the care system), and an illustrator, who met to explore an evidence-based intervention which could help to promote the welfare of 'looked after' children. The key component for the success of the project was that professionals worked together bringing their own particular expertise to develop ideas and support the project as a whole.

The idea of the project was to find a way to develop the emotional literacy of 'looked after' children. After discussions with children in contact with the care system it was decided to offer an intervention for all children, which was non-challenging and child friendly.

The hypothesis was that 'looked after' children's resilience could be best addressed through an intervention which targets all children, aiming to promote the well-being of all vulnerable children and their peers.

The first stage of the project was to identify and pilot a child-friendly tool, which could reach children and trigger a discussion on specific emotional issues. The multi-disciplinary team developed a visual image, a poster, highlighting a relevant issue for all children.

The posters are in the form of a cartoon and show the difficulties an individual might have in making friends or communicating with their peers at school. The posters are used in a variety of ways by the teachers according to the particular groups of children they are teaching. For example, some groups talk about the story shown in the posters, other groups act scenes that come from their discussion of the relationships shown. Some groups have cut up the poster and made single pictures from the cartoon sequence and written about each picture as a specific image.

The first poster considered a child's wish to be like any other child and the peer group response to a child who is perceived to be different. This poster was successfully piloted in four educational placements, mainstream primary and secondary schools, a special needs secondary school and the tuition centre for children who are out of school, many of whom have been in the care of the local authority.

After the initial pilot the project was developed further and a series of four posters was presented during the academic year. Each poster was developed from the one before, enlarging and expanding on the responses from the children in all the settings.

Teachers involved in presenting the posters had a training day with professionals from health and education. There was a sharing of ideas about the posters and ways to present them that could stimulate responses from the participants. After each poster was delivered in the educational settings the teachers met together with other professionals to share their experiences, look at the new poster and consider ways of working with it.

Each educational setting delivered the posters in an appropriate part of the curriculum and at a time best suited for their particular curriculum. The children's responses were recorded with their permission and this was used in the planning of new posters.

The aim of the Hopes Project was to provide early intervention to help emotional literacy in children in school, with the active participation of their teachers. The aims of the poster presentations were:

- That children will acquire expressive skills.
- That children's imaginative understanding will be enhanced.
- That children will be able to practice and enhance their narrative skills.

The project is to be evaluated through a series of questionnaires for teachers and pupils and through analysis of the children's responses to the posters. It is hoped that the children involved in the project will develop skills in the use of language to express emotions and share empathic understanding about the issues presented in the posters.

The play therapist working on this project was able to define objectives for the poster presentations with other professionals and participate with ideas of play and drama, which could develop from the images in the poster.

Conclusions

Play therapists have a variety of roles in the many settings in which their work can be a support to children. The key task is to offer therapy to children if this is appropriate and safe in the ecological environment in which the children are living. Sometimes it is more of a help to explore ideas of support with the adults who care for children. Another key role for play therapists is to explain their work to other professionals and help develop understanding about ways to talk and play with children, putting the children first.

The Apaches tell how curing ceremonies began. This is their story.

The Origin of Curing Ceremonies. An Apache story
This is how ceremonies started among us for the curing of sick people.

Long, long ago, the earth was made.

Then the One Who Made the Earth also planned for each person to have a piece of land that he could live on and call his own.

Our people were living in one such place, but they didn't like that particular spot.

So the One Who Made the Earth told them to move to a new location, and when they did, they slept well, and liked it, and lived in a good way.

Then two men among them became sick and became weaker day by day.

The people didn't do anything for them, because no one knew then about illnesses and how to cure them.

The One Who Made the Earth said, 'Why don't you do something for those two men? Why don't you say some words over them?'

But the people had no knowledge of curing ceremonies.

Four men among the people happened to be standing, one to the east, one to the south, one to the west, and one to the north.

The One Who Made the Earth spoke to one of these men telling him 'Everything on earth has power to cause its own kind of sickness, make its own trouble.

There is no way to cure all these things.'

Now this man understood that knowledge was available.

Then those four stood there.

On the first night, the one standing on the east side began to chant a set prayer all by himself.

On the second night, the one on the south started to drum and sing lightening songs.

On the third night, the one on the west chanted a set prayer.

On the fourth night, the one on the north began to drum and sing lightening songs.

They did not conceive this pattern in their own minds; it was bestowed upon them by the One Who Made the Earth.

It was as if the knowledge of what they should chant or sing had suddenly been transmitted to them from outside.

Then the One Who Made the Earth said to these four, 'Why don't you go to the two sick men and say some words over them and make them well?'

So those four went to where the sick men were and worked over them and they were cured.

From that time on we had curing ceremonies and knowledge of the different kinds of sickness that may be caused by various things.

That's the way all curing ceremonies started.

Chapter 6

Helping children through difficult life events and with chronic conditions

This chapter describes two play therapy interventions, one individual intervention with a girl waiting for an adoptive placement and a group intervention with children diagnosed with ADHD and/or depression. These show how play therapy can be a helpful way of exploring both life events which are stressful, and issues for children with chronic difficulties. They are examples of the kind of working which might be part of a play therapist's role.

MOVING TO ADOPTION

I met Rachel when she was four. She had come into care because her parents were unable to look after her. They had their own battles with drink and drugs. Rachel had lived in chaotic circumstances and during her short life had been parented by a large number of adults. There were two adults whom she considered to be her mothers and several males whom she had called father. Nurture had been haphazard depending on the circumstances of the adults with whom she lived. There had been no protection for her and very limited understanding of her needs as a child.

Rachel felt safe in her foster family although she found it difficult to keep to the routines of family life. Initially she did not miss the adults who had cared for her but she did miss her elder brother and sisters who were fostered elsewhere. The relationships in her birth family had been confused, her two sisters aged eight and ten and one brother aged nine had a mix of biological parents and had moved in and out of care when adult relationships shifted and care for the children disintegrated.

Rachel was offered play therapy to help her settle with her foster family and ultimately move to a family who would adopt her. We would focus on the themes that Rachel presented in play. She was articulate and could use the toys to sequence stories, which she liked to tell to me. She loved to play and enjoyed all our work together. She was quite clear about how she wanted the sessions to proceed and what toys she liked and wanted to use in play. She enjoyed small family dolls and small monsters and set them up in family groups, then told me what was happening. She loved play-slime and liked dunking small adult dolls and monsters into the slime. She often created a river or lake with the slime. This lake was sometimes a scary place, not often safe. Her first story was constantly repeated, adapted and amended. The theme of wanting adults to 'be good' was one which Rachel repeated again and again.

> Once upon a time there were two men from space.
> They were stuck in slimy stuff.
> Rachel and Ann got them out.
> One man was very cross and he shouted,
> 'Get me out,' in a very cross way.
> Ann asked him if he was cross and he said, 'No.'
> Ann asked the other space man if he was cross and
> The two men stayed on earth and be good.

She then made the slime more like a lake.

> *The Lake*
> The lake is breaking and fixing again.
> All the creatures get out for a while
> Because it is breaking again.
> The lake has serpents.
> One of the snakes goes back in the lake.
> He is nice.
> A lizard goes in and another lizard.
> Lot of frogs go in and they are nice frogs.
> They don't spit.
> A nice space man goes in.
> A frog jumps out of the lake.
> He got trapped in the lake but got out.
> But it was hard.
> 'Get me out' he shouted.
> There is a mum and dad, children and a baby.
> They are nice.

Her final story in that first session was called 'The Cross Mum'

The Cross Mum
There was once a mum and she got very cross
Because she didn't like getting married.
All the children are scared
Because they didn't know what she might do.
So they all hid.
Everybody hides and she is alone in the lake.
And she is shouting
'I don't want to get married.'
She gets out of the lake
Into the sea and she is stuck.
Now everybody can go back to the lake because she is gone.
Sometimes the mum is there, sometimes not.

Rachel wanted to play 'for ever'. The themes of her stories contained the worries and confusions which were part of her life. What was 'good' and 'bad' about adults and children. What it is like to be abandoned. Missing her past life. She expanded the stories as we played together and began to include ideas learnt from her foster family.

The following story explores the theme of a caring family.

Once upon a time there were two children
A boy and a girl.
The girl is called May and the boy John.
They have a nice mum and dad.
They did nice things together.
They did good work at school and watched TV.

She immediately went on to describe the naughty mum and dad. There seemed to be safe places and dangerous places in her world.

The naughty mum and dad
Live in the river.
Animals go in the river.
The animals swim in the river.
It is cold.
The monster is eating the mum,
But she gets away.

He is hungry.
He eats slime because he likes it.

She explored the theme of naughty adults and nice adults further and began to express what makes adults nice and what is scary.

The Naughty Monster
Once upon a time there was a monster
Who was very naughty to little girls.
There was also a nice monster and another horrible monster.
He licks the little girl's bottoms
And they don't like it.

Sometimes the 'good' people are in the scary places and no circumstances are clear-cut.

The Scary River
There is a ghost in the water.
And a fish caught it with his tongue.
The fish is grown up and a mummy.
She has a diamond in her tongue.
She is a nice mummy.
[*I asked what that means.*]
She puts you to bed in the river where you live.
She goes to bed on her own.
Naughty mummies shout.
Here comes a snake in the river.
The ghost was scared.
He thought that the snake would get him.
The snake just slithered off in the rain.
He is a bad one.
He jumps out of the water and just slimes around the floor.
He grabs a little girl and puts her in the water.
The fish mother gets her out.
He mustn't touch her on the head.
The big monster comes along.
And he eats the river.
He swallows it and spits it out.
He is biting his tongue, poking it and screaming.
He is eating more and more and more of the river.
He eats all the river.
The End

The New River
The new river is a nice river.
It's a friendly river.
The other monster tries to pick a bit up
And swing it around.
But he can't do it.
The End

Rachel begins to yearn for her birth family and tells a story expressing this feeling. The attachment she has to past carers is ambivalent but the feeling of loss is still strong.

This is the earth and it goes round.
The alien came out of the earth.
The mummy alien was swimming in the river.
She is looking for her children.
She is mad.
She is a lot mad. [*angry*]
The dad is talking to the alien.
He is a nice dad.
The children go to their mummy.
They want to go if they can get the slimy stuff off her.
The naughty dad is gone in the earth
Because he is naughty.
He hurt the children.
Hurt them by hitting.
He hit them hard.

Rachel liked me to tell stories and at this time, I told her a mermaid story, which she really liked because it expressed the loss she felt.

The Mermaid of Kessock
A man was walking along the shore near the ferry. He was beachcombing, looking for bits of timber and iron bolts. It was a long time ago. As he looked he saw a mermaid in the shallow water. He waded into the water and tried to catch the mermaid by pulling some of the scales from her tail.
It was thought that if you pulled off a part of a mermaid's tail she had to stay with you.

And before his eyes the mermaid was transformed into a beautiful girl, tall and fair, with long silky hair and beautiful blue eyes. And in place of her fish-tail she had slim white feet. The man fell in love with the mermaid and married her. He carefully hid the scales he had taken from her tail in the outhouse.

They lived in a cottage within the sound of the sea. Year after year went by and things were going well for them. They had children and seemed happy.

But when the mermaid heard the sound of the sea she longed to return to her home under the sea.

She pleaded with her husband saying that if she returned they would have a plentiful supply of fish and none of his family would drown near the ferry.

But her husband loved her too much to let her go.

One day one of the children discovered the scales in the out-house and took them to her mother.

Her mother was so happy to see the scales.

She said goodbye to her children, she told them she would be away for a while but they would never be short of fish.

She told the children to look out for her.

She kissed the children and went away.

She took the scales and went back to the seashore where she became a mermaid again.

They never saw her again but sometimes the family found a pile of fish on the rocks and it is said that at night people of the village heard a crying sound as though the mermaid was looking for her children.

It is also said that the mermaid still watches over her descendants and keeps them from perils at sea.

Stories came flowing out from Rachel about bad mummies and daddies. Descriptions of physical violence when the children were hit and stamped on, stories of drinking and stories of sexual abuse.

Rachel begins to think about a new family but still feels the sense of abandonment and shame about her past.

There was a horrible witch
The witch flies on the back of the dragon.
The dragon likes witches.
She has left her children at home.

The little girl sits on the witch's shoulders.
She is hanging upside down with her legs hanging.
She is the witch's daughter.

The boy is looking for his family.
He is riding his bike.
His family have thrown him out.
They didn't like him.
They were horrible to him.
They hurt him.
That's why he has his bike.
He cannot remember how his family hurt him.
So he gets on his bike and tries to ride it.
He only has the slime to look after him.
He has left his other family.
But he finds his pet and two families to look after him.
They are nice.
They won't harm him.
He doesn't want to tell people what his horrible family did.
But he is happy with his new family.
He remembers his old pet but now he has three pets.
He is going to tell his new family what his old family did to
him and his pet.
He won't tell the witch who was his mother or his old dad.
The witch gets stuck and falls down a mountain.
She hurts her bottom and falls in the slime.

Rachel is preparing to go to a new family and aspects of her play
and stories reflect this.

The big bad wolf ate the pig in the straw house
A Pokemon killed the wolf.
But he came alive and ate the other pigs.
All the Pokemon are cross with the wolf and the old daddy.
The old wolf is legging it home.
The old daddy is going to Mars.
The Pokemon be angry with the old daddy.
The old dad is trying to find McDonald's.
The old dad gets dead.
All the Pokemon are dead
Killed by the naughty boy.

He told his mum and she sent him up to his room.
One of the Pokemon is still alive
And goes to the wolf's bedroom.
She is angry at him.
She kills him.
She did it because all her friends are dead.
The old dad is trying to find McDonald's.
The Pokemon are still dead.
They start to get alive again.
The old witch's spell can keep the Pokemon dead.
Her spell makes the wolf come alive again.
'My son, I've missed you,' the witch said
'But I don't belong to you.
I belong to my mummy wolf.'
In the end the Pokemon are happy.
They come alive.
They all lived with the wolf
Who had learnt to be kind
And didn't eat pigs.
The dad is happy.
He finds McDonald's.
The old dad has no children anymore.
And the witch hasn't.
They couldn't look after them.
They are sad.
The children are a little bit sad.
But a big bit happy
Because they have a new mum and dad
The witch and the wolf live together.
All the Pokemon are watching them
Be down resting.
The End.

Rachel finally left her foster family after two years. She was adopted by a family who had a 10-year-old boy of their own. After a few months in her new family I visited her and continued to see her and her new brother together for six months. I then had some meetings with her new parents to help them with ideas to secure their attachment to Rachel.

It was difficult for Rachel to leave her foster family and much more difficult for them to let her go. Her new brother found sharing with her quite a problem and everybody had to adjust their lifestyle to accommodate a new person in the family. Rachel found the new family rules hard to learn and it was a shock to have a new brother. Her adoptive parents had to struggle with Rachel's angry behaviour and were shocked about how angry they sometimes felt.

When I first went to see Rachel in her new family we played together with her brother then I had some time to play with her alone. As time went on and Rachel found her place in the family, she asked if she might share all her time with me together with her brother. They both liked to play and make up stories with the toys and they enjoyed each other's stories and listened very well to each other. It was a struggle for both Rachel and John her new brother to find a way to become brother and sister and for both to manage their anger at having to compromise to make the attachment.

Rachel still missed her birth family although she saw all her siblings from time to time. We place great demands on 'looked after' children and perhaps don't acknowledge the strength of feeling experienced by many children when they lose not only parents but also siblings, other family members and pets. Rachel was often worried about the well-being of the animals she left behind when she came into care.

Conclusion

The play therapist can help a child on their journey into adoption by offering a safe, contained space for thinking about the loss of a birth family. There is also a need for the child to make sense of the new families she may encounter on the journey. It is hard to understand rules of family life for the first time and each family has their own way of organising their life.

Rachel's story continues. She is settling with her adoptive family but there are struggles to attach and sadness about the loss of her birth family. Her new brother has struggled with his feelings but now expresses great loyalty towards Rachel. The parents are getting over the shock they felt about the intensity of their feelings of helplessness as well as affection when Rachel first came into their family. There are good days and bad days but hope, always hope.

Rachel liked this story called *The Lass Who Went Out at the Cry of Dawn*. She thought that she was like the lass in the story. She liked the strength of the lass and her loyalty to family and the optimism of the story.

The Lass Who Went Out at the Cry of Dawn

There was once a lass who went out at the cry of dawn to wash her face in the morning dew to make her skin soft, and she never came home again.

Her father went looking for her and her mother cried but all the searching and all the crying didn't bring her back.

She had a younger sister who said that she would go out and search the world for her sister and she wouldn't come home until she had found her.

So her father gave her his blessing and a purse with gold inside. Her mother made up a packet of things for her. There was a bobbin of yarn, a paper of pins, a silver thimble, a gold needle, and a small sharp knife all wrapped up in a white towel. Her mother also gave her blessing.

The lass wandered the world asking for news of her sister. Someone told her that there was a wizard who lived on Mischanter Hill and he stole young girls and maybe he had the lass's sister. So off she went to Mischanter Hill.

When she got to the hill she discovered it was steep and rocky all the way.

So she sat down to rest a bit before she tried the climb.

While she was sitting there, along came a tinker. He was pulling a cart loaded with pots and kettles and pans. He stopped and called 'Good day.'

'You must be tired,' said the lass, 'pulling that cart.'

'Well,' said the tinker, 'I can't afford a horse so I must just go on pulling the cart with my load.'

'Well now,' said the lass, 'I've a piece of gold my father gave me and I've never had need of it. Take it and buy yourself a horse.'

The tinker thanked her. He said that she was the first person he had met who had given him a kind word let alone a piece of gold.

'If you are going up the hill to the wizard's castle I'll give you a few words to take with you. What you see and what you hear are not what they seem to be. My advice is not to go but I doubt you will heed that.'

'That I won't,' said the lass, 'but thank you kindly for your words.'

So the lass began to climb the steep hill.

When she was about halfway up the hill she met a poor ragged bodach. [A bodach is a fairy servant.]

His clothes were all ragged and he was trying to mend them with thorns.

The lass told him she had a paper of pins, which her mother gave her. 'Take them and do your mending with them.'

The poor bodach took the pins and said 'I've stood here many a day and nobody has given me a kind word. I have nothing to give you in return but a few words you might take along with you if you are to meet the wizard. Gold and silver are a match for evil. If I were you I would not go to the wizard's castle, as he will lay a spell on you. But I doubt you'll take my advice.'

'That I won't but thank you kindly.'

When she got to the castle she opened the gates and went right up to the castle door. She knocked and the wizard himself opened it to her.

As soon as she saw him she knew who he was because there was such evil in his face.

He asked her what she had come for.

'I'd like my elder sister, I hear you've brought her here.'

'Come in,' said the wizard, 'I'll see if I can find her.'

He took her into a room and left her there and shut the door behind him.

All of a sudden she heard flames crackling and the room was filled with smoke.

And she remembered what the tinker had said. 'What you see and hear is not what they seem to be.'

So she paid no heed to the smoke and it went away.

She sat back in her chair and waited again for a while.

Then she heard a voice. It was the voice of her sister calling and weeping.

She was ready to run and find her sister when she remembered the tinker's words again.

But the voice went on calling and she was desperate to follow the sound but she knew it was the wizard's magic so she took the bobbin of yarn from her packet and bound her arm to the chair until all the yarn was used up. Now she was safe for no matter how she pulled, the yarn held fast.

After a while the voice stopped and the lass took the small knife and cut the yarn to free her arm.

The wizard came back and was surprised and not too pleased to see her still sitting there. He told her to come along to another room because there were a lot of girls in the castle and she could pick out her sister for herself.

They went along to another room. There was nothing in this room but seven white statues and every one was the image of her sister.

'Pick your sister out,' said the wizard with a wicked smile. He thought that she'd never be able to do it.

The lass walked up and down the line of statues until she remembered the words of the bodach, 'Gold and silver are a match for evil.' So she took the silver thimble out of her pocket and slipped it on the finger of the first statue.

The thimble turned black as coal on all the statues until the last one in the line. 'I'll take that one,' she said to the wizard and as she spoke the statue moved and there was her sister turned back to flesh and blood.

The sisters held hands and went out of the room down the hall and through the door of the castle.

The wizard was furious and he magicked a great wolf and sent it after them.

The sisters ran faster and faster but the wolf caught up with them.

Then the lass remembered the bodach's words 'Gold and silver are a match for evil.'

She whipped the gold needle out of her pocket and turned to face the wolf.

She thrust the needle between his great red eyes and that was the end of him.

He dinged down dead.

The wizard in great fury came after the sisters.

The lass had only the small knife left to use and as she put her hand in her pocket to get the knife it somehow got tangled up with her mother and father's blessings.

And as she aimed the knife at the wizard the blessings carried it straight to his heart and down he fell, black cloak and all.

Then they heard a great noise and saw the castle crumble before their eyes.

The two sisters had no need to run anymore.

They walked down the mountain together.

Halfway down they met a fine young man dressed in the best of clothes.

'You'll not remember me but I am the ragged bodach to whom

you gave your paper of pins. The wizard laid a spell on me but now I am free.'

The three of them walked down the hill together and they met a fine young man standing beside a grand shining coach.

'I'm the tinker that you gave the purse with the gold piece in it. The wizard had laid a spell on me and now I am free of it.'

The four of them got into the coach and drove home.

So the younger sister brought her older sister home as she said she would.

The older sister married the fine young man with the pins and the younger sister married the tinker and they settled down together and lived happily ever after.

The End.

A PLAY THERAPY GROUP FOR CHILDREN WHO HAVE BEEN DIAGNOSED WITH ADHD AND/OR DEPRESSION

Introduction

One of the areas of work for play therapists is with children diagnosed with Attention Deficit Hyperactivity Disorder (ADHD). ADHD refers to a group of behaviours that can make children perform below their optimum level at school and at home. The problems often become noticeable during the first years at school although parents experience difficulties in the years before school.

There are three main symptoms which define ADHD; these are inattention, impulsivity and in some cases hyperactivity. Without hyperactivity it is usually called ADHD-Inattentive type or ADD. For the symptoms to be clinically significant and fulfil the diagnostic criteria they must be present in a significant number and to such a degree that the person's ability to function is significantly impaired.

The medicalisation of children's behaviour

Professionals who work with children are inclined to use a medical model to classify children's behaviour and it is important for the play therapist to think about their work and the ways we objectify children by using labels and classifications. In our work with children we need to continually evaluate what we do and to think about the narratives which are placed on children's behaviour by adults.

Historical and theoretical contexts

The behaviour of children and young people has been an enduring focus of concern by adults. The character and form of these concerns have changed as constructs of childhood have shifted, but the legitimated power and authority of adults to define what is appropriate and acceptable behaviour for children and young people remains constant.

Goldson (1997) states that the professionalisation of childhood and the emergence and development of discrete specialisms – each with its own corpus of knowledge and power – demands, maintains and reproduces a process whereby doctors, psychiatrists, psychologists, teachers, social workers and the like, have been able to penetrate and regulate the social world of the child.

A range of theoretical models of human behaviour have developed within and between the various academic and professional disciplines and professional practice has evolved within and has been shaped by the overarching application of the medical or disease model. This has shifted the explanations of human behaviour from a moral framework to an illness framework.

Coppock (2002) states that resistance to adult control is not considered a legitimate option for children and young people and can lead to their behaviour being pathologised, medicalised or criminalised depending on the arena in which it occurs and the professional discourse within which it is constructed.

This is not to say that challenging behaviour in children and young people is not problematic but it could be argued that the medical model is not always a reliable indicator nor an appropriate response to the distressed behaviour of children and young people.

The emergence of ADHD as a medical condition

Child (1996) states that there has been a powerful media-driven campaign to publicise ADHD originating in North America. Media descriptions of ADHD convince parents that it's their child to a T, leading on to pressure for diagnosis and cure by medication.

Ideus and Cooper (1995) give a cultural perspective on the origins of the ADHD 'epidemic', highlighting the particularly North American values of individualism, conformity, competitiveness and medical and insurance marketisation that feed the campaign there to establish and fund the labelling and special treatment and education of diagnosed children.

Child states that the attraction of a curative pill, e.g. Ritalin, has swung public and psychiatric diagnosis towards ADHD and away from other categories (e.g. conduct disorder).

Prior to the emergence of publicity about ADHD in North America, insurance companies were seeking treatment for children's behavioural difficulties from clinical psychologists and therapists as a cheaper alternative to child psychiatrists and paediatricians. However, only those with medical qualifications could prescribe medication so the control of treatment for ADHD still stays within the medical profession.

Coppock (2002) states that the rapidly expanding diagnosis and pharmacological treatment of ADHD is a worrying indication of the increasing social control of children and young people through medication, amounting to a breach of their human rights.

Ritalin is one of the drugs used to treat ADHD and UK statistics from the Department of Health in 2000 show an increase from 2000 prescriptions in 1991 to 14,700 by 1995 and 158,000 by 1999. It is estimated that by 2000 some 190,000 children in the UK were given psychiatric drugs to control their behaviour.

The majority of children and young people undergoing 'treatment' have not given their informed consent. It is the parents or other adults acting on their behalf who have given permission for them to be treated, an adult-led process to which the child or young person is expected to submit and conform.

Breggin (1998) reveals that children's and young people's views on the use of Ritalin are rarely sought and there is no comment in the literature on 'what the children themselves feel about any aspect of being diagnosed and drugged' (p. 82).

The child's right to medication

It has been argued by those who support the use of medication to help children that to deny a child access to Ritalin or other like medications is denying the child the right to treatment and this could impact on the child's successful integration into school and their social world.

Conclusions

The majority of narratives about ADHD present negative images of a child with such a problem. There is pressure on parents to control their children's behaviour. The 'cure' is the responsibility of the child and family, there is no real thought about how school and society in general might change to accommodate the needs of the children.

In 'The child as project and the child as being', Hallidan (1991) described the contrast between child-as-project and child-as-being. At home both are important but child-as-being is often dominant, and there is negotiation, while at school child-as-project holds sway. Children experience school as much more controlling than home.

The medical profession and pharmaceutical industries have a vested interest in 'cure' by medication. Medication is effective for many children and helps to keep them in school, however, there is limited consultation with the children about the kind of help they want for themselves. There is little information about how children feel about themselves or what it is like to have the label of mental illness attached to their behaviour.

> We claim to be a child-centred society, but in reality there is little evidence that we are. In many ways we are a ruthlessly adult-centred society where children are defined almost exclusively in terms of their impact on adult lives. Our adult-centred society has tried to contain and limit the impact of children on adult life by either excluding them from much of it [or] blaming them for disturbing it.
>
> (Mental Health Foundation, 1998, pp. 4, 5)

The behaviours

There are clusters of behaviours which form ADD/ADHD but not all children with ADD/ADHD exhibit all the behaviours listed.

Inattention The child is easily distracted, forgets instructions, flits from task to task and has poor short-term memory. Some children cope by becoming dreamy and distant.

Impulsiveness   The child speaks and acts without thinking and has a very short fuse. Often blurts out answers before questions have been completed.

Over-activity   The child is restless, fidgety, fiddles and touches things inappropriately.

Insatiability   The child is never satisfied, goes on and on, interrogates, intrudes and generates great tension.

Social clumsiness   The child is 'out of tune' socially, acts silly in a crowd, misreads social clues, overpowers and bosses, loses friends.

Poor co-ordination   The child may be clumsy, with physical movement lacking in flow, finds it difficult to do two actions at the same time, and produces messy written work.

Disorganisation   The child is unaware of mess, has problems organising schoolwork, and cannot get started on projects or homework.

Variability   The child suffers from mood swings, has unexplained good and bad days, can be volatile.

Problems with learning   These can include difficulties in reading, spelling or maths, speech and language difficulties and problems with handwriting.

These behaviours would have an onset prior to seven years of age, have a duration of at least six months, and be evident to a degree that is impairing development.

A child with some of these difficulties can wreak havoc at home and school. I was once working with three children diagnosed with ADHD in a room with a large window. A fire engine drove past in the road outside and all three children flung themselves at the window screaming and shouting, completely forgetting what they were doing. It was the extremity of the response which was so noticeable as they clambered up the window, walking over each other. We had been talking about difficulties at school with teachers becoming exasperated by their lack of attention. I suggested somewhat wryly as I picked them off the window and each other, that such an event could in future, be part of the diagnosis for school problems! We thought it should be called *Test 3 Response fire engine bell*. And although we laughed together, the impulsivity of their behaviour, their lack of care for each other, was dangerous. I wondered how they might react if they were outside, perhaps running across the road without looking to get near the fire engine. I also felt great sympathy and admiration for the teachers and carers who daily care for children who put themselves and others at risk of harm in unpredictable ways.

Causes of ADHD

There are a variety of discourses about the causes of ADHD.

A bio psycho-social disorder

There is no single cause for ADHD but there is a growing consensus that ADHD results from a chemical imbalance in the attention centre of the brain and this prevents the child from concentrating, planning and controlling their activity levels and their emotions.

Some new research has suggested that ADHD is not a disorder of attention per se, but arises as a developmental failure in the brain circuitry that underlines inhibition and self-control. This loss of self-control in turn impairs other important brain functions crucial for maintaining attention, including the ability to defer immediate rewards for later greater gain.

Genetic links

It has also been established that a child with ADHD is four times more likely to have other family members with the same difficulty but biological factors only predispose children to behave in certain ways.

Environmental factors

Environmental factors also play a part. The social environment, family and school may also contribute to the child's inattention and overactivity.

Numerous researchers suggest that both individual differences in the organic and psychological make-up of the child and individual differences in the family and social environment contribute to whether or not a child is identified as ADHD. This indicates a complex interaction between the child's environment and his or her physical and psychological status.

Disorder of adaptation

Jensen and colleagues (1997) published an interesting paper exploring the concept of ADHD in relation to evolutionary theories of biology and psychology. In evolutionary terms there are advantages to possessing the symptoms of ADHD in specific circumstances. The child with ADHD is defined as a 'response-ready' person:

Hyper vigilant with the ability to retrieve and integrate information through all of their senses at once
Rapid scanning
Quick to pounce (or flee)
Hyperactive (foraging for food, moving towards warmer climes as seasons and ice-ages come and go)

The 'response-ready' person is at an advantage in brutal or harsh physical conditions. In a hunter-gatherer society a response-ready person is a successful warrior. Jensen considers that in an industrial society these characteristics are less advantageous.

Viewed from an evolutionary perspective the school environment is most challenging for such a 'response-ready' child. By reframing a disordered child with ADHD as experience-seeking, alert and curious, and adapting their environment to suit their abilities, the child and family could perhaps cope more easily. This of course is easier said than done. However, there are still many activities which require the skills of the 'response-ready' person. Such careers as accident and emergency workers, rescue workers, soldiers, entrepreneurs. I know what kind of adult I would take with me on a short walk in the Scottish Highlands where I live if I needed to be hauled out of the snow.

Assessment for ADHD

Assessments for ADHD must be carefully made. It is all too easy to label any child with difficult behaviour as having ADHD but sometimes symptoms are ignored and no assessment made. For example, a 'looked after' child may not receive help because the difficulties are put down to their life circumstances, which may be part of the problem but not all. Social workers have told me that they don't 'believe' in ADHD but you don't have to 'believe' as it isn't a religion.

At the Child & Family Service where I worked, assessments for ADHD are made at a special clinic organised once every three months. The approach to assessment is multi-disciplinary and the team at the assessment clinic is made up of child psychiatrists, clinical psychologists, clinical nurse specialists, paediatricians, and a play therapist. The team reviews the child's symptoms, and their medical, educational, personal and family histories are taken. Reports and tests from a variety of sources are also considered. There is a meeting of all the professionals who have seen the family at the clinic so that information is further shared before the assessment is made. Children diagnosed with ADHD were then regularly monitored and parents offered support and the opportunity to join a Parenting Group if they felt that would be helpful.

The play therapy group

As a play and dramatherapist I offered to run a small group for children who attended the Service. The aim of the group was to use Drama and Play to enhance the children's self-esteem. It was to be a short-term intervention. The majority of referrals were for children diagnosed with ADHD.

The group was to meet for one and a half hours with a break for refreshments. We met for five Wednesday afternoons. The professionals at the Service were really pleased that I could offer a group for such children. I did note that the referrals were for children with very complex needs. In many cases the parents were in despair and welcomed any support for their children.

I took four children: three boys aged 10, 9 and 7 and one girl aged 7.

One of the boys, Ronnie, did not have a diagnosis of ADHD but was anxious and worried about his family and found separating from them and going to school very difficult. This made peer relationships difficult as he was always worrying about his family when he was away from them. There were many family stories about losing loved ones so all relationships within the family were held together with worry and anxiety.

James was quick, vital and very noisy. His difficulties were at school as he had great difficulty understanding social relationships.

He wanted to dominate and control all relationships. His parents almost certainly both had ADHD. They were both very like James, quick, vital, noisy and disorganised. This meant that they were also chaotic about appointments and timekeeping, which created anxiety for James.

Peter was diagnosed with ADHD and had difficulties at school where he was frightened of making mistakes. He responded aggressively with angry behaviour. At home his mother was exhausted through managing his behaviour. He was very impulsive, cutting through conversations and answering questions and instructions before they had been given. His usual response was 'I can't' 'I won't' before he knew what was being asked. He was very interested in aspects of history and had a vast knowledge of the life and times of Napoleon Bonaparte. Like James he was very noisy and shouted a lot.

Mary had been diagnosed with ADHD and other neurological complications from birth trauma. She had a limited understanding of social interactions and was often disinhibited in her behaviour. She was quick at remembering information but afraid to play. She was impulsive in her reactions to others in the group and afraid of being thought foolish.

The structure of the sessions

As we met for the first time it was clear that new experiences created fear and anxiety for everyone. Responses were extreme. Peter howled and sobbed and hid in the corner, James jumped around the room kicking the furniture, Mary giggled and screamed and Ronnie was shocked and astonished by the others. He wanted to be as noisy as they were but didn't dare.

The noise was to cover fear and when quiet was achieved the group members were amiable. There was little anger, just worry about what was expected of them. The meaning of our meetings and being in a group had to be explained in great detail. Group rules were eventually established. You don't have to play if you don't like the game but stay with the group in the room, show respect for each other and the furniture and me. Group members liked a predictable structure but found rules difficult to understand. It was soon clear that the children needed the sessions to have a routine form and this had to be simple and clear. Each week we went through the structure until everybody understood and felt comfortable. Through trial and error it became clear what kinds of social interactions, games and play were tolerable for everybody.

The routine each week began with sharing stories about the past week. The stories were mostly about school and the information, which created group cohesion, was their fear of school and their lack of understanding about rules and expectations. One of the reasons they liked the group was because they didn't have to be at school.

There was a great sense of relief that the entire group felt the same fear of school. There were stories about getting into trouble, being told off by teachers, being bullied by other children. All negative representations. Ronnie gave a lot of help to the others about the meaning of school. His fear was different from the rest; his was about separating from his family and what might happen to them while he was away. He had a good understanding about the social meaning of school as an institution. Ronnie could explain to the rest of the group what was expected of pupils at school and to hear the information from another group member was more helpful than being told by an adult.

Children with ADHD are often talked at or shouted at by adults and their response to this is total panic or refusal to listen for fear of making a mistake. Ronnie was able to explain to the others why the teacher or another child was irritated or angry with them. He was imaginative and supportive and gave them good strategies to manage in social situations. In doing this he also gave himself some good ideas.

After the conversation and information sharing at the beginning we had some partner games. Initially I tried whole group games but this proved too stressful so we changed to games in pairs. This part of the session was most difficult for Peter. He found any new instruction or experience very frightening. As I explained a game and how to play it, he responded by cutting through the talk, crying, hiding his face and wailing 'I can't do it, I don't understand.' He was very reactive and impulsive when given an instruction. We thought about this together and with help by relaxation and counting up to five, he learned to hold his anxiety and evaluate an instruction before complete panic set in.

The group liked repetition of successful games and as fear subsided individuals began to suggest partner games for each other. Mary began tentatively to suggest partner games, which she played at home with her mother. James and Peter were impatient with her but Ronnie was very sympathetic and defended her until the two boys listened. Mary really liked being the centre of attention with something to tell to the others.

The games we played with partners were concentration games, or simple imaginative activities in pairs. For example:

Change three things

Partners sit on the floor and face each other.
Partner 1 thinks about the way they are sitting.
Partner 2 looks at Partner 1 and remembers how they are sitting and what they are wearing.
Partner 2 closes eyes.
Partner 1 changes three things about the way they are sitting or what they are wearing.
For example, unfolds arms, moves watch to other arm, pulls up sleeve of jumper.
Partner 2 opens eyes and tries to guess the three things which have been changed.

Tasks for two people

Find something that needs two people to work together like folding a sheet or taking a splinter out of a finger.
When you have chosen mime to the rest of the group.

Can you do things together?

Can you skip with your partner?
Can you move back-to-back around the room with your partner?
Can you crawl through a hoop without letting go of your partner's hand?
Can you be very small with your partner?
Can you sit face-to-face with your partner and row a boat?

These games were very popular and often repeated. Instant success is very rewarding. It is important to evaluate the level of concentration in the group before deciding which games are possible and won't end in mayhem.

Ronnie gained in confidence. He became aware that he had skills, which he could share with the others, which could help them be more successful in school. He liked the freedom in the group and especially the noise and shouting and energy, which the others had in abundance. He could explain the rules to Peter if he was in a panic. He had been reticent and fearful but in this group he could be noisy. He began to take on some of the characteristics of the ADHD children, which he found very liberating. He became noisy and impulsive but stayed creative. At the end of the afternoon, when the group ended, he abandoned the role of child with ADHD and became calm.

After the games in pairs we had a break with a drink and biscuits. This break was very important, perhaps the most import-ant ritual of the meetings. Members of the group used food and drink as a way to communicate with each other. They could talk more easily if they were eating or drinking and they didn't have to make eye contact. They also had a good topic of conversation, which was the food and drink. Each week they discussed the quality of the biscuits and graded them in order of deliciousness. I had to choose different biscuits each week. The drink must always be Sunny Delight in individual bottles. I checked with parents that the food and drink were appropriate for their children.

Mary began to prepare for the break at least five minutes before time because it was so important for her. 'Is it time yet?' she asked. It was her treat and she enjoyed the ritual. At first she wanted to eat and eat and drink more than anyone else. I discussed this with her mother and we decided to let her make her own decisions and eat what she wanted. Her greed soon subsided when she could make her own choices without being nagged. She began to dis-criminate between biscuits and was able to criticise my choice and decide which she liked to eat and which were not so appetising. She didn't like plain biscuits but enjoyed custard creams, which she could take apart.

It was interesting to watch the group start the break. There was a sense of relief when the games were over even though they had enjoyed themselves. There was always that sense of dread that they would be asked to do something or be with someone in ways they found difficult to understand. Then came the break and everyone relaxed. I went to the kitchen to prepare the drinks and biscuits and the group followed in crocodile line watching my every move, then walked back in line with their drink and biscuits. Then they began to talk to each other. They were able to converse and mediate their relationship with each other through talk about the food. They were nurturing each other, which they found difficult at other times. Food was easier than the games because there were fewer rules to remember so less worry. This was the only time that the group members were cohesive in their communication and recognised they were a group.

After the break the group used toys and other objects to play and make stories. In the beginning I tried to suggest some whole group drama or play but they found this impossible and it was clear that developmentally only Ronnie was able to understand the meaning of dramatic play and storymaking as a group. They were not able to play together but played as individuals enjoying the presence of the rest of the group, as small children needing each other but not able to share. They chose toys for themselves, mostly construction toys, building garages, bridges and the like. Only Mary was able to role-play and she often chose the doctor's set and a doll to examine. She was a strict doctor telling her 'patient' how to behave and what to do.

We used this time to learn some sharing skills. Negotiating was difficult, tempers often flared. Responses to each other were exaggerated, either flinging their arms around each other or sulking and crying. The arguments were about who had what piece of equipment and they often destroyed each other's buildings in the way of two-year-olds. The behaviour was impulsive, 'I want it now' was the cry regardless of the needs of anyone else. We tried techniques of waiting, negotiation, and as time went on they learnt some respect for each other and to quieten their exaggerated responses.

We ended each session with a quiet relaxation, if possible, but endings brought their own anxiety for each of them. The group was over; they cut through the ending with their minds on what happens next. They found it difficult to wait their turn to exit from the room. They jammed the doorway together like characters in a silent comedy film. Were their parents there to collect them? Were they going anywhere special? Everything and everybody forgotten, they sped away.

This was the most difficult time for James. His parents had his impulsivity and often were not there to collect him after the group. Sometimes they forgot the time, or their attention was taken by another task. They always came for him but never on time. When I spoke with them about James's anxiety at the end of the sessions they understood but found it rather odd.

The group ran for five sessions. All members attended all the sessions except James whose parents found it difficult to remember to bring him and forgot twice. Saying good-bye to each other in the final session was difficult. The problem was, as always, finding an appropriate level for communication. Mary flung her arms around Ronnie saying she loved him. He responded sensitively, disentangling himself with a loving smile. Peter managed to say good-bye without crying and hiding. They all asked for the group to be repeated because they liked the time there and they liked each other. Ronnie in particular had found that the group released him from sadness, he felt useful to the others, and found being noisy better than being angry. Mary had found companionship with the others who hadn't mocked her although they all squabbled with each other. Peter discovered that he could achieve if he gave himself time to listen and that his knowledge of Napoleon was very impressive and he could share that and people would listen out of genuine interest. James had discovered that other people of his age could like him if he listened to them a bit more.

After the group ended, I wrote reports for the parents and met with the family and the referrer from the clinic. It had been very useful seeing the children interact with each other and I was able to offer suggestions to the parents and referrers to help the children negotiate relationships from the work we had done in the group. I was able to shift the narratives about the children by describing the progress they had made and the qualities and skills they presented in the group rather than focus on all the negative stories that were circulating about the children.

Conclusions

The group was exhausting and would certainly have been less so with a co-worker, which had been in the original plan. I made a list of my thoughts about the planning and organisation of the group.

Planning and organisation
1. *Important to accept the group as individuals not as the labels attached to them.*
    Although the children experienced difficulties especially at school, they were interesting individuals with qualities and gifts of great value to society. I enjoyed their company however

exhausting, impulsivity can be creative as well as chaotic, and most of all we had fun.

2. *Need for structure and certainty in the routines of the group.*
   All the children had anxiety about what was expected of them so the clear routine and sequencing of activities in the group lessened their anxiety. They still worried about their social behaviour but less so as they met more often and the routine was established.

3. *Need for group rituals and repetitions which reinforce successful achievement.*
   Rituals and repetitions were important in helping the children gain self-confidence. If they achieved skill in a game with a partner it was important to repeat it immediately and during the following weeks. The ritual of sharing food was important in securing group confidence.

4. *Need for basic nurture and acceptance.*
   All the children had been hurt by comments from other children and adults about their behaviour. The children's own limited empathy (with the exception of Ronnie) did not inure them to the insults of others. They did manage nurture with food and were able to share information about how difficult they found their lives at school.

5. *Finding a good mix of group members to help each other.*
   A small group is essential when there is impulsive behaviour and joint working appropriate. It was very helpful to have Ronnie in the group because he was able to interpret social behaviour of their peer group. Careful selection of group members can be helpful. A large group of inattentive, impulsive children could be disastrous and exhausting for both facilitators and group members.

6. *Importance of family support.*
   All the families of group members wanted this support for their children and this was most helpful for the children and myself. James's parents found it difficult to organise bringing James to the group but they wanted him to be there.

7. *Importance of contact with the family and referrers after the group has ended.*
   It was helpful to the families to know the children well enough to be able to talk to parents about their skills as well as difficulties. Parents often feel oppressed by the negative criticism of their children and many are exhausted by the task of

keeping their children safe. Mary's parents could never be off their guard because she was so impulsive and disinhibited so they felt nurtured themselves when they heard good things about their daughter.

Group learning

1. *Children had limited imaginative play as individuals with no group social play.*

   The children with a diagnosis of ADHD seemed stuck on the play continuum at an early stage in the development of imaginative play. They enjoyed construction play but could not develop this into imaginative play except in a limited way. They found imaginative social play with each other impossible and although Mary could role-play it was only as an individual not with others. By the end of the sessions, the group members were learning to share with each other and could tell a simple story about the buildings they had created with the toys and bricks.

2. *Impulsive behaviour response to instruction or information sharing.*

   Initially group members responded to an instruction about a game with reactive behaviour based on fear of not understanding. 'I don't want . . .', 'I can't . . .' As the group continued, individuals could be helped to hold on to their feelings and listen rather than explode their fear. Techniques of relaxation were important for this purpose.

3. *Problem solving.*

   It was important to recognise the level of understanding of group members. The group was not able to function socially as a whole group using imaginative play so problem solving took place in play with partners, group conversations about school and home, and sharing of food. It was important to develop confidence and a relaxed atmosphere so the children didn't feel 'blamed'. Then the children were able to listen, negotiate and solve problems if they thought it useful to do so. The meanings of some social interactions were not understood but they would want to learn the behaviour if it brought acceptance and friends.

Recommended reading about adoption

Fahlberg, V. (1991) *A Child's Journey through Placement.* London: BAAF.
Parkes, C., Stevenson-Hinde, J., Marris, P. (eds) (1991) *Attachment Across the Life Cycle.* London: Routledge.

Recommended reading about ADHD

Barclay, R. (1998) *ADHD: A Handbook for Diagnosis and Treatment*. New York: Guilford Press.

Fletcher, J. (1999) *Marching to a Different Tune*. London: Jessica Kingsley Publishers.

Green, C. (1994) *Understanding ADD*. Australia: Doubleday.

Jensen, P., Mrazek, D., Knapp, P. et al. (1997) 'Evolution and revolution in child psychiatry: ADHD as a disorder of adaption', *Journal of the American Academy of Child and Adolescent Psychiatry* 36(12): 1672–1681.

Munden, A. and Arcelus, J. (1999) *The AD/HD Handbook*. London: Jessica Kingsley Publishers.

Chapter 7

Play therapy and therapeutic play

In this chapter I describe some views about the importance of imaginative play for children and offer some suggestions of games and stories to stimulate play as a way for adults to start to make connections with children. I then describe a way of playing for refugee children which I wrote as part of an information pack.

Playing together with children

The Glass Ball

There was once a woman who gave to each of her daughters, a beautiful glass ball.

The girls loved their glass ball, but one day while they were playing with them, one tossed her ball over the wall into the next garden.

This garden belonged to a fox, who didn't like to play and who never talked to his neighbours.

The girl was very much afraid of the fox, but she went to the door and knocked, and the fox came to the door and said she could have her ball back if she would serve as his housekeeper for one year.

Unwillingly she agreed, but the fox made her very comfortable and happy until one day he said to her, 'I am going away and until I come back, there are five things you must not do. You must not wash up the dishes, sweep the floor, dust the chairs, look into the cupboard, nor under my bed.'

The girl promised, but when the fox had gone, she began to wonder why he had given her such strange orders.

Soon she washed the dishes to see what would happen and a great bag of copper fell down in front of her.

Then she swept the floor and a great bag of silver fell down in front of her.

So she dusted the chairs and down fell a bag of gold.

She looked in the cupboard and there was her glass ball.

At last she went upstairs and under the bed lay the fox.

Terrified she ran downstairs and out of the house, until she came to a lane.

At the top of the lane she met a horse and she said,

'Horse of mine, horse of mine,
If you meet a man of mine,
Don't say that I've passed by.'

And the horse said 'I will not.'

Further on she met a cow, then a mule, then a dog and a cat and an owl and to each of them she said the same thing and got the same reply.

The fox followed close behind and he said to the horse.

'Horse of mine, horse of mine,
Hast thou met a maid of mine?'

And the horse said 'She just passed by.'

The cow, the mule, the dog and the cat all gave the same answer.

'Which way did she go?' said the fox to the owl.

'You must go over the gate, across the field and behind the wood you will find her,' replied the owl.

So the fox ran off, but neither he, nor the girl nor the glass ball have been heard of since.

This story described the delights of a beautiful toy and the dangers and adventures you might experience if you chase after it. The story describes an imaginative and curious child who is learning about life through her adventures. I wonder if the fox caught her or she made an escape. I think she is a survivor and will outwit the fox in some way.

Playing with children, using toys and dramatic play, telling stories together, is in itself a very therapeutic process. For many children who have lost family, friends, or are uncertain about their lives, a relationship with an adult who can play with them is the best form of recovery. Many children will not want to expose their distress through therapy but they can achieve pleasure and joy through play with an adult, which does not pressurise them.

The way we perceive play has changed over the years. Sutton-Smith (1994) describes the many adult interventions in children's play, in public play with the development of organized sports and playground provision and in private play where we have intervened with toys, with television. He suggests that if our interventions are genuinely playful or allow children their own genuine playfulness then we will go beyond the rhetoric about the paradigms of childhood. He suggests that as it stands, we are typical hypocrites who pretend that children play and that we adults do not.

It is interesting to think about Christmas and how during the past few years there has been one desirable toy, which parents must buy for their child to prove themselves 'good' parents. Shopping to prove love can be an adventure for the adults, perhaps a displacement activity to avoid actually playing with children.

Characteristics of play

Johnson and colleagues (1987) describe five characteristics of play that help us understand the process.

1. Play is characterized by a play frame that separates the play happening from everyday experience. Within this frame the internal reality of 'playing' takes precedence over external reality.
2. Play motivation is intrinsic and comes from within the individual, and activities are pursued for their own sake.
3. Play defines the importance of process over product. When children play their attention is focused on the activity rather than the goals of the activity. This creates an absence of pressure that tends to make play more flexible than goal-oriented behaviour.
4. Free choice is an important element of young children's understanding of play. This seems to be less important as children grow older.
5. Positive affect. Play is usually marked with signs of pleasure and enjoyment but even when it is not so pleasurable,

children still value the activity. Some play activities cause apprehension for the child, like climbing to the top of the slide but the repetition of such activities suggests there is some pleasure in being afraid.

(Johnson et al., 1987, p. 12)

Play is an important part of the child's world. It is the place where experience is structured. The activity is special and enjoyable even when 'daring deeds' are part of the activity.

The idea of being scared but still feeling safe could be the same as feelings associated with listening to a scary story, first being scared then controlling the fear. Repetition is important here. The first time we hear a scary story there is the added tension of not knowing what happens in the end but once the story is familiar then we are still scared but in a more controlled way. Sometimes we can imagine alternatives. The story of *The Glass Ball* offers us our own choices about what happens to the girl so she can get back home or be eaten by the fox, whatever we want.

Sometimes a scary story can create a bond between storyteller and child with screams of fear then laughter and delight as the story ends. Repetition creates attachment through the shared experience. An exaggerated presentation with repeated lines to be shared with the child are an added bonus. I like *The Stove Worm*.

The Stove Worm

The length of the Stove Worm is beyond telling, and the Worm reached thousands and thousands of miles in the sea.

His tongue was hundreds and hundreds of miles long, and it would sweep whole towns, forests of trees, and huge hills and mountains into the sea.

The tongue was forked and he used the prongs to seize his prey.

He would crush huge ships like an eggshell.

He would crack the walls of the biggest castle and suck every living thing out of it.

One time the Stove Worm set up his head near the shore, and the people had to feed him, every Saturday morning with seven young girls.

The people went to an old wizard for advice, and he said that if the king's daughter were given to the Stove Worm, the monster would leave them and trouble them no more.

The king was very sad because his daughter was his only child and he loved her very much.

He agreed but first he insisted on having ten weeks' grace.

He used the time to send to the countries around, offering his daughter and kingdom to anyone who could destroy the Stove Worm.

On the last day of the ten weeks the Master Assipattle made his appearance. In his boat he entered the Worm's mouth, rowed through the monster's gullet, set fire to the Stove Worm's liver, and returned to the land.

The liver being full of oil, blazed into a terrible fire, and the heat caused the Stove Worm great pain, so he almost capsized the whole world with his struggles.

He flung out his tongue and raised it far in the heavens. By chance he caught hold of the moon, and they say he shifted it in the sky.

He took hold of one of its horns, but by good fortune his tongue slipped over the horn. Down fell the horn and made the earth quake.

Where it fell, the tongue formed a great channel in the face of the earth, now filled with the sea, dividing Denmark from Norway and Sweden.

As the serpent lay struggling in great pain, he lifted up his head to the sky and then let it fall with a crash. As he did so, some of his great teeth fell out and they became the Orkney Islands. The second time he did this more teeth fell out and they became the Shetland Isles.

When he was dying, he coiled himself into one huge lump, threw up his head, and again it fell striking the bottom of the sea, the teeth were knocked out and became the Faroe Isles.

Then the Stove Worm rolled himself up, and his huge body when he died, became the large island of Iceland. But his liver still burns, and the flames of the fire are sometimes seen rising from the mountains of that cold land.

This story can be told with actions, repetitions, as the monster is tamed. These kinds of stories help children experience a fear but in the safety of a story told by an adult. There is a delicious pleasure gained from listening to such a tale and the shared fear between storyteller and listener creates bonding.

The functions of imaginative play

Pelligrini and Smith (1998) describe how mental and cognitive states develop through social fantasy play. Children discuss what a character might say. For example, 'doctors can't say that', so children learn to talk about language through playing and taking roles.

Another theory is that pretend play is an indicator of meta-representational abilities and these show as early as 18 months. Meta-representational abilities are one facet of the theory of mind and these abilities are critical for understanding that someone else may represent things (knowledge, or beliefs) differently from yourself. This is the beginning of empathic understanding, knowledge that not everyone thinks and feels the same as you.

Dunn (1987) states that fantasy play both alone and with parents and siblings starts as early as 24 months. She states that children show interest in other people in pretend play, in conversations with their parents and siblings, over stories and while watching television. She emphasises the importance in play of language and communication, cognition and perception for children in the development of social understanding and relationships.

Experimental deprivation studies

Some experimental studies have been conducted where children were deprived of an aspect of play like social play or physical activity play, the assumption being that if play is developmentally important, once deprivation has ceased then there should be a 'rebound effect' when play is resumed. Children would compensate for deprivation by engaging in higher levels and longer duration of play. Three sets of experiments with physical activity play showed that increased deprivation led to increased levels of play when opportunities to play were resumed (Pelligrini and Smith, 1998). This might indicate that it could be helpful for children who have been deprived of play opportunities to be offered extra opportunities to play, by themselves, with other children and with a supportive adult.

Playing with children

Sutton-Smith (1994) describes the increasing domestication of children's play, by which he means the increasing control and supervision of play to get rid of its physical dangers and its emotional licenses. This domestication has also led to moving childhood play indoors. This leads to control of who enters the house with play banished to the bedroom, so instead of 'go and play outside' the call is to go to the bedroom, watch TV or play on the computer. Play has become a more solitary activity.

I remember my own childhood when after school, I changed into old clothes and went to the 'rec' (Recreation Ground) where my friends and I (our gang) played with a very unsuitable group of boys who tried to grab our ankles when we were on the swings or climbing trees. There was no supervision of our playmates or our activities so long as we returned home at the required time and were reasonably clean. There was excitement at meeting friends and being chased by the other gang. It was an intense experience with no adult control but still with clear boundaries of what we could do without getting into trouble. No smoking, no kissing the boys or some terrible retribution would happen.

I now live in a small village and see children playing as I did as a child. Ball games, marbles in the season, skipping; gangs playing in the road, screaming and shouting and fighting and playing. Going home in tears to 'tell on you' then out again to rejoin the gang. The children inhabit the street and control the traffic; they sit on the garden walls and plan adventures together.

I think with some sadness of the children I met in London where play outside was not a real possibility. I remember a Jamaican mother talking about the freedom to roam, which she remembered from her childhood, and the loss of that joy for her own children stuck inside a flat on the tenth floor. To go out to play means a walk to the park with the activities managed by adults. Meeting friends has to be arranged by adults so everything is contrived and formal.

Then there are school pressures, a life of tests, with artistic activities allotted to after school time. I speak with children whose diaries are frantic, tap dancing Monday, violin lessons Tuesday, sea cadets Wednesday and so on. A life organised by adults, busy but perhaps lonely. No wonder some children use their computers as the place where they can control the play and use the equipment with a skill unknown to adults. You can have adventures there.

Helping children and families with play activities

Sometimes adults find it difficult to play themselves so it is often helpful to suggest ideas about play to adults to start them off playing with children. This can also be true of professional workers who talk *at* children with no idea of reciprocal play as a way to communicate.

I have structured this section to examine three themes and look at a game, a story and recommend a book for each theme. The first theme is attachment play, then running and chasing and finally reflection.

Attachment play

A game

COOING AND SMILING

The first play between mother/carer and child is the reciprical response to cooing and smiling. Baby coos and smiles and mother responds with cooing and smiling in exaggerated form.

PEEK-A-BOO

Adult and child make face-to-face contact.
Adult or child initiate hiding by one putting hands over face or putting cover/cloth, scarf or whatever over the face.
(At this time each can ask 'Where's Jane?' or 'Where's mummy?' and so on.)
Then the hidden one uncovers their face.
Play ends with the remaking of contact between the two.
There are many variations to this game. It can be played sitting down or moving about. The uncovering can be done by the other player or the person covered.

This kind of play is universal for adults with babies and small children and is a way to create attachment by reciprocal play. Some mothers who had difficult childhoods might find it a struggle to play in this way and will need encouragement and support.

A story

This story, in a similar way to Peek-a-Boo, is a question and answer story and comes from the Arctic region. It is also a

nonsense story with no logic. There are many stories like this one.
You can make up your own on a similar pattern.

The duck whose grandmother was out of her wits
There was a duck who called herself White Cap.
She asked her granddaughter to louse her.
'Oh grandma there are no lice on your forehead but plenty on
the back of your head.'
'Quack, quack,' said the old woman in duck language, 'there
are none on the back of my head but plenty on my forehead.'
'Oh grandmother why do you talk like that? You never used
to.'
Quack, quack,' said grandmother. 'I always talked like the
grey geese that pass high above me.
They have made me lose my wits.'
The girl was frightened and ran away.
She was alone and sat down on a high stone.
Along came the snow bunting bird and perched on a cranberry
bush.
The girl asked it
'What do you want?'
The bird replied singing and talking,
'Pititti do you feel warm?'
'I do feel warm.'
'Pititti why do you not bathe in the river?'
'I am afraid I might drown.'
'Pititti why do you not hold onto a willow?'
'I am afraid to get a splinter in my palm.'
'Pititti why don't you put on mittens?'
'I'm afraid they'll get torn.'
'Pititti why don't you just mend them?'
'I'm afraid the needle might break.'
'Pititti why don't you just sharpen it?'
'I'm afraid the sharpener might slip and my brother would
blame me.'
'What is your bed?'
'A dogskin.'
'What are your spoons?'
'Dog's paws.'
'What are your forks?'
'Dog's claws.'

'What is your kettle?'
'Dog's skull.'
'What is your sledge?'
'Dog's cheekbones.'
'What are your ladles?'
'Dog's shoulder blades.'
'What are your cups?'
'Dog's teeth.'
'And where is your fire?'
'A jay flew by and blew it out.'
'And where is the jay?'
'It flew away into the mountain to pick larch-gum.' The End

A book

There are many picture books for children about family life. I like *Tell me Something Happy Before I go to Sleep* by Joyce Dunbar and Debi Gliori (1998). Willa the baby rabbit finds it difficult to sleep. Her brother suggests she thinks of something happy and together Willa and Willoughby think of all the happy things waiting for Willa in the morning. Good to read of siblings helping each other, even rabbit siblings!

Running and chasing play

Many children who have experienced difficulties cope by being 'response ready' all the time and their energy levels are very high and not well focused. Running and chasing games in the park encouraged by a supportive adult can help children lose some of their surplus energy which in other circumstances, at home, exhausts adults and at times wrecks the house. (The adults shouldn't play, just encourage the children to run faster, otherwise everybody will be exhausted!)

A game

GAMES OF TIG

Chasie   Two equal sides each of any number. One side runs away the other side chases after them until they catch every one. There is no den.

Tig   One person is 'it' and chases the others. You start with 'Tig, you're 'it'' and the tigger runs away and the game starts.

Aeroplane Tig   The person who is 'it' chases the others and when one is tigged they are to stand still with their arms out like an aeroplane. If one of the free ones tigs this one, he can be freed. The first person to be tigged three times is 'it' in the next game.

Hospital Tig   When you are tigged on the eye, head, arm, leg, etc., you have to hold that part of your body with one hand as though you were hurt, and you have to go about like that and try to tig somebody else.

Windmill Tig   The person who is 'it' stands with their back to the others with their arms waving up and down. The others have to run and get under the arms without being touched. If they are touched they join the person who is 'it' and start waving their arms too.

A story

This is a short adventure story with a fair bit of running about.

> *The Cat and the Mouse*
> The cat and the mouse,
> Play'd in the malt house.

The cat and the mouse were playing chasing in the malt house and the mouse was tired of being chased and slowed down a little.
And the cat bit the mouse's tail off.
'Pray, Puss give me my tail.'
'No' said the cat,
'I'll not give you your tail, till you go to the cow, and fetch me some milk.'
> First she leapt, and then she ran,
> Till she came to the cow, and thus began:
'Pray cow, give me milk that I may give cat milk, that cat may give me my own tail back again.'
'No' said the cow, 'I will give you no milk, till you go to the farmer, and get me some hay.'

First she leapt, and then she ran,
Till she came to the farmer and thus began:
'Pray farmer, give me hay, that I may give cow hay, that cow may give me milk, that I may give cat milk, that cat may give me my own tail again.'
'No' said the farmer, 'I'll give you no hay, till you go to the butcher and fetch me some meat.'
First she leapt, and then she ran,
Till she came to the butcher and thus began:
'Pray butcher, give me meat, that I may give farmer meat, that farmer may give me hay, that I may give cow hay, that cow may give me milk, that I may give cat milk, that cat may give me my own tail again.'
'No' said the butcher, 'I'll give you no meat, till you go to the baker and fetch me some bread.'
First she leapt, and then she ran,
Till she came to the baker and thus began:
'Pray baker, give me bread, that I may give butcher bread, that butcher may give me meat, that I may give farmer meat, that farmer may give me hay, that I may give cow hay, that cow may give me milk, that I may give cat milk, that cat may give me my own tail again.'
'Yes' said the baker, 'I'll give you some bread,
But if you eat my meal, I'll cut off your head.'
Then the baker gave mouse bread, and mouse gave butcher bread, and butcher gave mouse meat, and mouse gave farmer meat, and farmer gave mouse hay, and mouse gave cow hay, and cow gave mouse milk, and mouse gave cat milk, and cat gave mouse her own tail again!

This is nice to act.

A book

There is a picture book called *What If?* by Joanna Walsh, which is about fears of imaginary dangers and what you would do if, for example, you met a dragon on the way to school. The drawings are strong and the 'what if' ideas full of fun. There is a lot of running away. Or alternatively Barry Smith's (1991) *A Child's Guide to Bad Behaviour*, which lists all the things that children can do to drive adults crazy. Lots of fun!

Reflective play

A game

In this instance the game is a book called *Nina's Book of Little Things* by Keith Haring (1994), which has lots of illustrations and space for drawing and writing. For example a big drawing of a blue purse and a page to draw or write about the things you would like to put in a blue purse (if you had one). Keith Haring's drawings have an immediacy which is very appealing and to write and draw in the book is a real luxury.

A story

This is an Ashanti story from Africa, a tall tale relaxing to tell with a smile at the end.

> *Talk*
> Once not far from the city of Accra, a farmer went out to his garden to dig up some yams to take to market.
> When he was digging, one of the yams said to him,
> 'Well at last you're here. You never came around before to weed me and now you are here with your digging stick.
> Go away and leave me alone.'
> The farmer turned around and looked at his cow in amazement.
> The cow was chewing her cud and looking at him.
> 'Did you say something?' he asked.
> The cow kept on chewing and said nothing.
> But the man's dog said,
> 'It wasn't the cow that spoke to you. It was the yam.
> The yam said to leave him alone.'
> The man became angry because his dog hadn't spoken to him before and he didn't like his tone of voice.
> So he cut a branch from a palm tree to whip his dog.
> Just then the palm tree said,
> 'Put that branch down.'
> The man was getting upset about the way things were going and was about to throw the branch down.
> Then the branch said,
> 'Man, put me down softly.'

He put the branch down gently on a stone and the stone said, 'Hey, take that thing off me!'

That was enough and the frightened farmer started to run for his village.

On the way he met a fisherman going the other way with a fish trap on his head.

'What's the hurry?' the fisherman asked.

The farmer said,

'My yam said, "Leave me alone," then the dog said, "Listen to what the yam says!" when I went to whip the dog with a palm branch the tree said, "Put that branch down!" then the palm branch said, "Do it softly!" then the stone said, "Take that thing off me!"'

'Is that all?' the fisherman asked.

'Well' the fisherman's fish trap said, 'Did he take it off the stone?'

'Wah,' the fisherman shouted.

He threw the fish trap to the ground and began to run with the farmer.

On the trail they met a weaver with a bundle of cloth on his head.

'Where are you going in such a rush?' he asked them.

The farmer said,

'My yam said, "Leave me alone," then the dog said, "Listen to what the yam says!" when I went to whip the dog with a palm branch the tree said, "Put that branch down!" then the palm branch said, "Do it softly!" then the stone said, "Take that thing off me!"'

'And then,' the fisherman said 'the fish trap said, "Did he take it off?"'

'That's nothing to get excited about, nothing at all,' said the weaver.

'Oh yes it is,' said the bundle of cloth. 'If it happened to you, you'd run too!'

'Wah,' the weaver shouted and began to run with the others.

They came panting to the ford in the river and found a man bathing.

'Are you chasing a gazelle?'

The farmer said,

'My yam said, "Leave me alone," then the dog said, "Listen to what the yam says!" when I went to whip the dog with a palm branch the tree said, "Put that branch down!" then the palm branch said, "Do it softly!" then the stone said, "Take that thing off me!"'

'And then,' the fisherman said 'the fish trap said, "Did he take it off?"'

The weaver wheezed, 'And my bundle of cloth said, "You'd run too."'

'Is that why you are running?' said the bather.

'Well you'd run in their position,' said the river.

The bather jumped out of the river and began to run with the others.

They ran down the main street of the village to the house of the Chief.

The Chief sat in front of his house to listen to their complaints. The first man said;

'My yam said, "Leave me alone," then the dog said, "Listen to what the yam says!" when I went to whip the dog with a palm branch the tree said, "Put that branch down!" then the palm branch said, "Do it softly!" then the stone said, "Take that thing off me!"'

'And then,' the fisherman said 'the fish trap said, "Did he take it off?"'

The weaver wheezed, 'And my bundle of cloth said, "You'd run too."'

'And the river said the same' the bather said hoarsely, his eyes bulging.

The Chief listened to them patiently but couldn't stop from scowling.

'Now this is a really wild story. You'd better all go back to work before I punish you for disturbing the peace.'

So the men went away and the chief shook his head and mumbled to himself,

'Nonsense like this upsets the community.'

'Fantastic isn't it,' his stool said. 'Imagine a talking yam!'

A book

Draw Me a Star by Eric Carle (1995) is a beautiful book about how an artist paints. The pictures are glorious with strong colours and images. It is peaceful to look at together with a child. An experience to share, especially before going to sleep or at other quiet times.

These games, stories and books give a structure to help adults think about ways of communicating with children. Any supportive connection through play can stimulate the child's and adult's imaginations and their empathy with others. The children learn the rules and structures of games and stories, which help give a feeling of containment and a sense of autonomy. Looking at a book together or telling stories to each other is a way to develop a rewarding relationship.

PLAY WITH REFUGEE CHILDREN

This section was written for a publication to support the care of refugee children and has more ideas about creative play with children.

Self-expression through play

Children's rhymes are part of their armoury to cope with the world and perhaps tell us, the adults, what they really think and feel. What Iona Opie (1992) calls 'a declaration of a child's brave defiance in the face of daunting odds'. This armoury is especially needed by those children who come to this country as refugees, trying to make sense of so many changes and losses. They may be angry, frightened or depressed and the attitude of some whom they meet here can only add to their distress.

Play and especially imaginative play is the place where children can express their defiance, confusion, sadness, joy and excitement and try to make sense of their own particular world and what it feels like to live there. They can play aspects of their lives and their experience of the world, through making other imagined worlds and in making sense of these created worlds come to terms with their own particular reality. This is the paradox of play, safe in the world of play we can declare:

Oh that I were where I would be,
Then would I be where I am not;
But where I am there I must be
And where I would be I can not.

And explore the loss of home in the safety of the playing space and the containment of the rhyme.

Trevor, a Romanian refugee aged 8, now adopted in this country, told this story with small toys set in a sand tray. I wrote the story down for him.

The Beach Scene
Now the dogs are back on the beach.
They meet the other dogs.
The mermaid was hidden away.
Her hair was hidden until she was buried.
Then the RSPCA man came back and checked up on all the dogs.
He also brought the operating table.
He must check up on all the dogs.
But one day a bad thing happened.
As the man was inspecting the dogs a big dump of sand came and buried him.
He was buried.
Nobody could save him.
Another man came and took the dogs away back to the centre.

Now all the family are back at home.
Grandad came to stay with grandma.
They want to see the children.
Grandma is playing games with the children.
One evening there is a big storm.
Grandfather is really scared.
All the babies are really scared.
They have lots and lots and lots of kids.
A big family.
They are English, Indian, Jamaican.
No Romanian children.
They didn't want them.
Now it is night time.
All the children are in bed.
They had to have a big big bed to sleep in.
There are so many children.
And the mum.
They all had their little toys.
Then they fell fast asleep.
The End.

It is only through play and the story that Trevor can explore memories of an orphanage, of children being sorted like the dogs in his story, and state his feeling that to be Romanian is somehow shameful. 'Nobody wants Romanians,' he says. And sadly this was at a time when newspapers and television were full of negative stories, which reinforced these feelings for him. Trevor couldn't talk about his world directly but was able to tell how he felt through his imaginary stories. He also liked this rhyme:

> All's done,
> All's said.
> To-night
> In a strange bed
> Alone
> I lie.
> So slight
> So hid
> As in a chrysalid
> A butterfly.

This helped him understand that others had felt like him and that he too like that lonely child could turn into a butterfly.

Play as healing

When we play with children and listen to their stories it is important that the comments we make are connected to the story, not to the child's reality world. Many of the themes of stories express the terrible pain of loss and rejection but the child needs the safety of the story to be able to express how they feel. For the child, to play in the presence of someone who listens and can share the meaning of the story, is a healing process. The child and adult establish a relationship together and they mediate this relationship through play. The purpose of the play and the relationship is to help the child make sense of their world through the narratives and stories, which emerge as the relationship and the play develop.

We use toys and play materials to make stories and narratives about past and present. We co-construct together. There is a storyteller and a listener and the story acts in the middle as a way to negotiate a shared meaning between adult and child. Children tell stories as containers for their experiences, constructed into the fictional narration of a story.

Framing the play

Bateson (1995) states that before engaging in imaginative play, children must establish a play 'frame' or context to let others know that what is happening is play, that it is not real. This is usually done by smiling and laughing. When children play they learn to operate simultaneously at two levels. At one level they are involved in their pretend roles and stories and focus on the make-believe meaning of objects and actions. At the same time they are aware of their own identities, the other players' real identities, and the real-life meanings of the objects and actions used in the play.

Children in play can flow from pretend roles back to their own identities then back again to their play roles with an ease which many adults lose. We adults try to distinguish 'reality' from 'fantasy' in a very crude way, not really understanding that two levels of awareness of roles can operate in very sophisticated ways.

Materials for imaginative play

There are three aspects of imaginative play, which are defined as the developmental play paradigm. These three play processes are called embodied/sensory play, projective play and enactment or role-play. These are learnt progressively and by two and a half most children use all three in imaginative play.

Embodied play

Embodied play starts when the small infant begins to expand their environment through sensory exploration. It is the way the child discovers where their body ends and the rest of the world begins. This kind of exploring, touching, smelling, sniffing, tearing things apart is apt to infuriate adults but is one of the great thrills of childhood.

Refugee children may have witnessed or experienced acts of violence which have led to a shut down of this kind of sensory exploration as a way of coping with terror and fear. This means that these children will have a limited body awareness for touch and taste. However, they may have needed to be hypervigilant so sight and hearing can be very sophisticated because watching what those around them are doing, and listening for their approach, could have been a matter of life or death. You need to watch out to survive, and the trick is to keep moving.

This old English rhyme tells children about another child who kept moving, showing that there is some universality about jumping around:

> Anna Elsie she jumped with surprise;
> The surprise was so quick, it played her a trick;
> The trick was so rare, she jumped in a chair;
> The chair was so frail she jumped in a pail;
> The paint was so wet, she jumped in a net;
> The net was so small, she jumped on the ball;
> The ball was so round, she jumped on the ground;
> And ever since then she's been turning around.

This is fun to play, pretending we have the objects required to jump around.

A great pleasure for a child in a safe relationship with an adult is to explore their environment through the senses, discovering the relationship of their embodied self to the rest of the space around them. This kind of sensory play can take place in complete silence, which can be restful and soothing.

Sometimes a Treasure Basket can help establish this trust between child and adult because no talking is required to enjoy the experience. Playing in the presence of a caring adult who puts the child's interests first is the beginning of trust and a way of bonding. This basket can be used once a baby can sit up but can be enjoyed at any age.

Treasure basket (devised by Elinor Goldschmied)

The basket should be about 36 cm across and 10–12.5 cm high with a flat bottom and no handle. The basket needs to be solid so it can be leant on without spilling, and should be filled with a collection of objects which encourage the senses:

Touch	texture, shape, weight
Smell	variety of scents
Taste	sweet, sour

| Sound | ringing, banging, scrunching, tinkling |
| Sight | colour, form, length, shininess |

Natural objects: could include fir cones, feathers, walnuts, pumice stone, shells, dried gourds, lemons, apples.

Objects of natural material: could include woollen balls, wooden nailbrush, shaving brush, bone shoe horn, wooden comb.

Wooden objects: small boxes, rattles, coloured beads on string.

Metal objects: spoons, toy trumpet, harmonica, bottlebrush, bicycle bell, bunch of bells.

Leather objects: textile, rubber: rubber ball, beanbag, lavender bags, leather purse.

Paper, cardboard: boxes, inside lavatory rolls, little notebooks, corrugated cardboard.

It is important to find special objects, which can remind children of their country of origin.

The role of the adults is to be attentive and available to the child, making sure the child is comfortable but there is no need to be active in stimulating the child to explore. This is a good example of playing in the presence of someone who is attentive and keeps the space safe for the child.

Sensory materials

The materials for sensory play are usually determined by place and availability. Sand and water, bubbles, play-doh, noise putty and megaslime, which is colourful, runny and messy. The function of this kind of embodied play is to allow the child a sensory exploration of the materials without any other purpose. This is a relief for children who might think adults want return for their interest in them. Children often use megaslime as a body fluid, for example, hanging a long piece from the nose or mouth, often as an exploration of what is 'me' and 'not me' and what comes out of me and can escape into the world.

Projective play

Projective play develops as the child begins to explore the world of objects and toys. Play with objects develops from simple action patterns when the infant grasps an attractive object and develops through the exploration and investigation of objects to sequences of more complex play. In these explorations the child learns that toys and objects can replicate things in the real world. Infants learn to invent objects which are not present and then transform objects so that one object can represent another. Thus a chair becomes a car, a saucepan a crown. The child then plays in the 'as if' mode.

In a play session with a child, there is often a move from sensory play to projective play and the child often uses megaslime to represent the 'mess' of life. J, aged 8, was playing with slime and took a monster toy and told this story:

> There was once a monster called Gaudi and he ate slime
> Because he had an appetite for slime
> He ate so much purple slime that it came out of his tongue, his mouth and his brain
> [J showed this dripping slime in the mouth of the monster as he narrated his story]
> And he was sent away to a country where people were hit and burnt and he was very scared so he ran away back to the slime country where he felt safe.

J was able to describe his journeys from country to country through his imaginative story.

Toys and objects

Toys and small objects should facilitate the telling of stories. They should form categories of heroes, villains, family groups, magical people, wild animals and domestic animals, mythical creatures, pre-historic creatures, earth-bound creatures and sea creatures including mermaids. There are trees, fences, bridges and other objects to make environments. It is important to have some of the current desired toys and be knowledgeable about current toy obsessions.

The toys which children like to use are not necessarily those adults like. Pretty wooden well-dressed family dolls are an adult's delight but not the children's; they like cheap and cheerful representations, which they can buy with pocket money. Perhaps the most popular are those toys and objects despised by adults or which shock and offend them, like noise putty which makes rude noises when squeezed. A sand tray is a helpful way to create an environment for the small toys. Buy a blue cat litter tray which is a good size for this kind of play. Blue is important as this can represent the sea when the sand is moved on the bottom. Place sand in the bottom about half the depth of the tray then toys can be placed in the sand. Some of these small toys and objects are not culturally appropriate for all children so it is important to talk with parents about what can be used.

Some cultures use sand or mud drawings to tell stories. For example, Yup'ik Eskimo children in Alaska use a 'place' on the riverbank to work the mud with their story knives using symbols drawn in the mud with their knives. This is a girl's special activity (play exclusive to girls); and the stories are the means by which young girls come to know their culture and themselves. These activities still continue as a cultural tradition alongside television. This kind of marking out play could be done in school or nursery using cornflour and spatulas to make pictures, which could tell a story.

It is important to find out if refugee children have any traditional games or play, which are important to use as it is through this kind of cultural routine that children learn their social identity and take pride in their history.

Games of hide and seek, mime and singing, have similar structures in all cultures, but with specific references to particular environments. For example, there is a Japanese song called The Lotus Flower:

> A flower opens,
> A flower opens,
> What flower opens,
> The lotus flower.
> As soon as it opens it closes,
> So swiftly that we are not aware.

This is repeated with:

> A flower closes,
> A flower closes . . .

The rhyme or song is spoken and the mime is done with the two hands cupped to represent the lotus, which open and close as described in the verse. There are many similar children's rhymes in different cultures. These rhymes and games can be used at school or by parents and children to re-establish bonding between adults and child.

Describing a life event using toys

Sometimes toys and objects can be used to help a child tell about a difficult experience and share it with their family. This would be a private story between child and parents or between child and trusted adult, perhaps a teacher, but not when other children are around.

S was a Somali refugee who lived with her mother, sister and two young male cousins. One of these young male cousins was traumatised by events he had witnessed in Somalia. He became psychotic and in this state he entered S's bedroom and attempted to sexually abuse her. Her sister who shared her bedroom called out for help and their mother came and stopped the abuse. Her cousins subsequently went to live elsewhere and S was kept safe. However, S had been very frightened by the experience and in discussion with her social worker, S's mother thought it would be helpful if S could describe what happened with the use of toys.

I met S, her mother and an interpreter who knew S. We all sat on the floor together and talked about playing this scary event. Nurtured by her mother and the interpreter, S began to choose some play figures to tell her story. She selected a small female figure to represent herself and a gorilla figure on all fours to represent her cousin. With the help of these figures S enacted the event and it was clear that the gorilla figure expressed very clearly what it felt like to be woken by this seeming monster on her bed. S enacted this story three times to get the details clear for herself. We all reinforced how brave she had been, how she had been kept safe by her family and how her future safety was assured by her mother. S and her mother hugged each other. It was important that S could tell her story in a way which kept her safe. She was supported by her mother who was the person S wanted to tell, and the relief at telling was clear. It also meant that S and her mother could talk again at home about the incident.

However, it is not always the case that children want to talk about distressing events. For some children playing the past is often a theme they wish to explore when they first begin to play.

Other children experience the opposite desire and are fearful of their memories and playing the past could create more fear. The adult stands with the child and offers her or himself as the safe companion for the child's journey, whatever that might be. If the past is chaotic, with no logic for what happened, no sense can be made of it other than to acknowledge the chaos and confusion.

Role-play

Children begin 'let's pretend' play with activities in which the role taken is to play themselves, then through experiments with toys and other children they eventually learn to pretend to be somebody else.

As children learn to play other people then they begin to involve themselves in role-play with other children and adults. By four years of age children can adapt and combine their role-play with the make-believe play of other children. A box full of dressing up clothes is a way to stimulate role-play about imaginary characters. To role-play everyday life events can be very helpful for refugee children to make sense of a new environment. A trip to the superstore can be played out with other children to understand what happens in a big store.

Setting up an environment for play and stories

Children like to play in special places set up for that purpose so a Play Room with toys and a sand tray and water is an excellent space for storymaking. It doesn't have to be a big space but somewhere away from the classroom where privacy can be assured.

If children have had very frightening experiences it is important to offer them a time to play either individually or in a small group.

Sitting together on the floor, or perhaps using a mat to sit on together and defining that area as the special playing space can help children feel safe and comfortable. It also delineates the space for play as separate from their reality world.

It is important to help children through imaginative play and not expect them to tell about past events, which are too painful to express. It is much safer for children to tell of their fears through imaginary stories, which is why folk tales and fairy stories are still so vibrant for children.

It is very important for teachers and nursery workers to keep the boundaries of play in the special place and not try to use what children play as a way to get them to talk about their past. The imaginary stories and play are healing processes in themselves.

If children are telling stories in play it is important for the teacher or nursery workers to write them down if the children want that. If children have to write their own stories it becomes school work rather than play and can be especially difficult for some refugee children who are struggling with the language.

If a child does tell a story of a past experience to a teacher or nursery worker it is very important to listen and respond in a genuine way to the narrative. If the child is distressed then give reassurance about the safety of their present environment. Adults often find children's pain difficult to bear and want to make it better rather than genuinely listen to what the child is saying.

Children who are experiencing specific distressing symptoms like constant nightmares, excessive fears, bedwetting or poor concentration, might need more specialist help from a therapist and could be referred through their GP or other agencies who might be involved with the family.

Conclusions

Imaginative play is the way children make sense of their experiences. It is important to support refugee children as they play and find meanings for complex life events in different environments. Children need to be heard; to play in the presence of someone who will keep the playing safe and respect the children's narratives. It is also important for the adults to be able to play and tell stories to children, which will place their experiences in a broad cultural frame. We need to empower children by listening to what they say, in the way children express themselves. I end with a story which has a message for all of us.

> *Spreading the Fingers, from Suriname*
> Long ago, Ba Yau was a plantation overseer. He had two wives who lived in the city. But he brought them provisions from the plantation as he found them.
> When he brought things he said to them, 'When you eat, you must spread your fingers.' But the first wife didn't understand very well what he meant.

He told the second wife the same thing and she understood. What he meant was that when he brought them things, they were not to eat them alone, but they were to give others half. Now the one who didn't understand, in the afternoon when she cooked, she ate. Then she went outside and spread her fingers and said, 'Ba Yau said when I eat I must spread my fingers.' Ba Yau brought her much bacon and salt fish, which she alone ate.

But when Ba Yau brought the things for the other one she shared half with other people because she had understood what the proverb meant.

Later Ba Yau died. But when Ba Yau was dead nobody brought anything to the wife who had spread her fingers for the air. She sat alone.

But to the other one who had shared things with other people, many people brought things. A cow, sugar, coffee. She received many things.

One day one wife went to the other and said, 'Yes sister, ever since Ba Yau died I have been hungry. No one brought me anything. Why have so many people brought you things to eat?'

Then the other one asked her, 'Well, when Ba Yau brought you things what did you do with them?'

She said, 'I alone ate them.'

Then the other one said, 'When Ba Yau said to you "you must spread your fingers" what did you do?'

She said, 'When I ate I spread my fingers in the air.'

The other one said, 'Well then the air must bring you things because you spread your fingers for the air.

As for myself the same people to whom I gave things, bring me things in return.'

So the proverb means when you eat you must eat with people, you must not keep all for yourself. Otherwise, when you have nothing, nobody else is going to give you, because you have not given people what was yours.

Chapter 8

Research in play therapy

Practitioners as researchers

Play therapists often have difficulties in describing their work to other professionals, and indeed clients, in language that is understood by everyone. If there is confusion about what happens in the therapy process, and outcomes are difficult to describe because the language is not shared, then the therapy can be undervalued.

It is important that play therapists should feel confident about describing and evaluating their work to others and that the structures they use for this process are acknowledged as valid forms of research. There is now a great demand for evidence-based practice for therapeutic work of all kinds and play therapists should be able to present their work to others in forms that evaluate their practice.

It is not my intention to write about setting up a research project describing design, methodology and applications, but to reflect on useful ways of thinking about practice. I will describe the use of case studies and hermeneutic research as approaches that can be used to reflect on practice issues. Two play therapists describe aspects of their research projects using these methods.

Robson (1993) describes a practitioner-researcher as someone who has a job in a particular area and at the same time carries out systematic inquiry, which is of relevance to the job. In these circumstances research can help the practitioner think about what happens during an intervention but also to research issues relevant to a particular work environment to see what changes might be made which will support the therapeutic intervention.

In all research around therapy interventions it is critical to consider that the therapeutic relationship exists in a 'protected space' and never undertake any research which violates that concept. The client's needs are paramount. It is often difficult to gain informed consent from children so it is especially important to gain permission from them and to explain what happens to the information discovered in the research. When I ask permission from children to use their stories, I explain that I will not use their name to protect their confidentiality. They often say that they want me to use their name and I have to explain very clearly why that is not appropriate. They are often disappointed when I stay firm.

Qualitative research

Both case studies and hermeneutic studies are qualitative research. This kind of research describes processes and changes over time. It is often contrasted with quantitative research, which identifies processes, how often they occur and what differences occur over time.

In *Doing Research with Children* (1999), Greig and Taylor describe the quantitative and qualitative frameworks for such research. They describe the *quantitative* research framework as being based on assumptions about the *objective* nature of children, knowledge and research methods. This approach is based on the scientific activity of deduction – the procedure for testing existing theory. This means that the quantitative framework requires a methodology in which theory exists and is tested empirically to be proven or not proven. The basic method for conducting quantitative research is experimentation.

The *qualitative* research framework is based on assumptions about the *subjective* nature of children, knowledge and research methods. This approach is based on the scientific activity of induction – the procedure for generating new theories and in which theory emerges from the data. The notion that theory emerges from the data is consistent with the view that the child is subjective in nature and that his/her understanding, knowledge and meanings are subjective and emerge in interaction with others in a given context. Hence the qualitative framework entails a methodology in which theory is 'grounded' in data such as observations, interviews, conversations, written reports, texts and their interpretations.

Meldrum (1998) states that qualitative research is much more about the author or the researcher. It is multi-method in focus, involving an interpretive, naturalistic approach to the subject matter. Qualitative research including case studies involves the use and study of personal experience, the description of events and primarily the meanings that people place on these phenomena set within the natural surroundings of the person or persons being studied. So the researcher uses a wide range of interconnected methods in the hope of getting a better understanding of the research question.

Janesick (1994) describes the characteristics of qualitative design as:

1. Qualitative design is holistic. It looks at the larger picture, the whole picture and begins with a search for understanding of the whole.
2. Qualitative design looks at relationships within a system or culture.
3. It refers to the personal, to the face-to-face.
4. It is focused on understanding a given social setting and not necessarily on making predictions about that setting.
5. It requires the researcher to become the research instrument. This means the researcher must have the ability to sharpen the skills necessary for observance and face-to-face work.
6. It incorporates informed consent decisions and is responsible to ethical concerns.
7. It makes room for description of the role of the researcher as well as description of the researcher's own biases and ideological preference.
8. Qualitative design requires ongoing analysis of the data.

Meldrum (1998) states that qualitative implies an emphasis on processes and meanings that are not examined or measured in terms of quantity, amount, frequency or predictability. Qualitative researchers stress the socially constructed nature of reality and the intimate relationship of researcher and the subject of research, recognising and addressing the constraints of the context or environment of the research which shapes the enquiry.

Case studies

Robson (1993) describes a case study as a strategy for doing research, which involves an empirical investigation of a particular contemporary phenomenon within its real life context, using multiple sources of evidence. This means that a case study is a research method which uses systematic observations and data collection, the research takes place within a specific environment and information about the case comes from a variety of sources.

Stake (1995) describes three kinds of case study:

Intrinsic case study: used when the researcher wants to understand more about a particular case and not because it represents other cases. It is of interest because of the intrinsic interest of that particular client in that particular setting.

Instrumental case study: used when a particular case might provide insight into an issue or refinement of a theory. The research is undertaken to give insight into the external interest.

Collective case study: the extension of an instrumental study to several cases when the researcher believes that understanding these cases will illuminate issues or aspects of theory.

Robson (1993) suggests that the quality of the case study depends to a large extent on the quality of the researcher. This work calls for a person who has an open and enquiring mind, who is a good listener, is adaptive and flexible, can interpret information not simply record it, and is as unbiased and unprejudiced as possible.

Meldrum (1998) suggests a series of questions to ask before starting a case study:

1. Why as a clinician are children referred to you?
2. Why do you want to do a case study?
3. Who is to be selected for this case study?
4. Why this particular child rather than another?
5. What are your research questions?
6. What is your time frame?
7. What data will you collect and from whom?
8. Which sources do you need to contact for information on the case?
9. Whose permission do you have to ask?
10. How will you engage with the ethical, consent and confidentiality issues and concerns?
11. What support and supervision do you have?
12. What methods will you use to store the data?
13. How will you assess the outcomes?
14. How will the data be analysed?

15. How do you write up the case?
16. To whom and how will the finished study be disseminated?
17. Any other questions?

A case study report

Alison Webster is a Hospital Play Manager who wanted to research the disruption caused by repeated hospital admissions for a school-aged child. She used a single case study as the core of the research. This research is practitioner research by Robson's definition, in that it is relevant to the work of the hospital setting in which the therapist works and also illuminates her own practice as a play therapist. The information from the research has been disseminated to staff at the hospital through presentations by the therapist and this has enhanced the relationships between hospital staff and children with chronic conditions who need ongoing care.

The following extracts are taken from the research.

Question

The question asked was as follows: Can a brief three-session intervention of play therapy help a school-age child to explore feelings of being able to cope (or not) with the disruption of repeated hospital admission caused by chronic health problems?

Abstract

A brief, three-session intervention of play therapy is used to explore themes of coping concerning hospitalisation. This is analysed through story-work co-constructed with a school-aged child who has a congenital urogenital malformation requiring life-long hospital care. Analysis is achieved through a triangulated research design using a variety of methods between the child, her family, play therapist and allied health care professionals. Previous research findings suggest that there are discrepancies in the literature biased towards a deficit-centred approach in understanding this group of children's needs. Impact of hospitalisation on this age group is found to have conflicting results, which this study seeks to explore further through a strategy using a single case study design.

Coping is viewed within a perspective of problem-solving and emotional management strategies, commonly held to be a theoretical model suitable in supporting this area of research. Results from this study would suggest that further thinking is needed in order to develop appropriate theoretical frameworks to help code children's story work more clearly. In doing so it is hypothesised that a meta-coping model could be utilised to help gain a better understanding of children's coping styles, which may also help in their therapeutic engagement with processes such as play therapy.

Social constructs theory is the theoretical basis underpinning the use of play therapy to help in an understanding of the child's sense of self and her relationships with other people – especially in the area of healthcare and home environments. It also provides the reflexive framework to aid in the play therapist's understanding of her own relationship with the child through the co-construction of the stories. Recommendations are made which include developing a specific coding framework for analysing children's stories and their coping constructs. This is seen in relationship to building preventative interventions using play therapy, and with identifying its use for school-aged children suffering difficulties from coping with any stresses caused by hospitalisation required for treatment of chronic health problems.

Aims of the study

A broad aim of this research project was to explore the use of play therapy through a referral of a child for one-to-one intervention within an acute hospital setting. Play therapy is not clearly recognised in this environment. It is often confused with the role of hospital play specialist, or the equivalent American profession of a child life specialist. This intervention was differentiated from that offered by the hospital play specialist because of its use of a specific play therapy paradigm, based on a written contract negotiated between the referring care-team, myself, the child and their family, within a research strategy accepted by the Health Authority's Ethics committee.

Within this acute sphere where time is limited in which to work with children through play therapy I considered the possibility of developing a brief, three-session play therapy model of intervention. Its purpose could be to contribute towards analysing how children view coping with hospitalisation within the context of how they perceive their world, expanding their psychosocial assessment prior to admission i.e. a potentially preventative intervention of psychosocial support. It could also serve as a basis for considering the use of further play therapy support during and after admission.

An 11-year-old child was referred for play therapy because there were concerns from the child's care-team and parents about how she was coping with her condition, with previous psychosocial support having been refused by the child. She was given the opportunity to explore her feelings, using the play therapy sessions as a child-centred medium with a focus on the theme of hospitalisation, rather than that of her illness. By exploring and identifying the themes arising through such play, specifically the theme of potential disruption through hospitalisation, I hoped to demonstrate whether it is possible to analyse the child's sense of coping using this intervention of play therapy. I hoped to make links through this analysis with her possible vulnerability towards hospitalisation. A central objective was to try and identify potentially 'camouflaged' feelings of being able to cope (or not), which may have become more visible through the use of metaphor and symbolic play contained in the stories arising out of each of the three sessions. As part of the hermeneutic design of this study, I explored a range of responses to the themes in these stories from other carers/health care professionals and the child herself, to see how widening perceptions of the stories could expand on understanding this child's feelings within the hospital context.

The underpinning theory to this research project is that of social constructivism. There were some key issues to consider, including problems such as identity, self, personality and personal agency – these being some of the contentious issues as yet unresolved within discourse literature. A sense of self within social constructs theory can be considered as an 'experience' and this sense of self must have a location in many places and in relation to others.

As a focus in this area of 'selfhood' I explored how a child has developed a discourse about coping with hospitalisation rather than with being ill. This in turn led to reflexive explorations of how a medical discourse conceptualises coping, using a hermeneutic design for analysis. I have considered implications for how I understand the child's views from the perspective of being a play therapist, and how my professional efficacy as an advocate of these views and needs may be heard, bearing in mind that I am a co-constructor within this therapeutic process.

Design

Through using a case study, some flexibility could be developed as a strategy, which is also realistic to the practical considerations of working within an acute hospital setting i.e. time restrictions and access to a suitable child . . .

A single case study allows for some detailed analysis of the content of collected data within a particular context. An important point to consider is Robson's (1993) view, that a case study is a strategy rather than a method, such as observation or interview.

Data collection

This was a triangulated, multi-method approach including the play therapist's views, the child's views and adults' views.

PLAY THERAPIST'S VIEWS

The play therapist's views included play therapy process recording and observations, and self-completed questionnaire, which incorporated themes analysis.

CHILD'S VIEWS

The child's views included self-reported test material, and a self-completed questionnaire.

ADULTS' VIEWS

The child was involved in deciding which adults should be given her stories and questionnaire. She agreed on the following staff: paediatrician, hospital play specialist, senior nursing development practitioner, clinical psychologist, play therapist, clinical nurse specialist, European consultant for Action for Sick Children. Some of these adults were known to the child, others not known.

Adults' views included set questionnaires and self-completed questionnaires.

This approach was to help validate the data from the case study, improving its accuracy and to provide a measure of reliability in the findings through using a variety of sources. It was also possible to look at cross-validating any correspondences and to examine any discrepancies as they arose in the data.

Conclusion

In drawing conclusions arising from the analysis of this study, I pose a number of questions:

Can this study illustrate whether play therapy provides fresh alternatives for supporting school-aged children's needs who have to cope with hospitalisation for a chronic health problem?
Are such insights able to have generative potential?
If so – then what new narratives could be developed in a health care model for supporting these children?
Could play therapy be seen as a potential strategy for preventative intervention in supporting developmental difficulties caused by the impact of hospitalisation on these children's lives?

I have specifically looked at the area of school-aged children's needs when coping with hospitalisation caused by a chronic health problem. Through the literature review I have found that such children face the potential for being vulnerable to these experiences, but that previous research into how they cope within such an environment shows conflicting findings, leaning towards a deficit-centred bias of maladaptive coping. It would also seem that the developmental frameworks used to identify such difficulties may globalise children's needs, with little relevance being attached to cultural, social or historical aspects of these assessments. Further to this, a medical view of coping seems biased towards an outcomes focus, i.e. success or failure of a child to cope, which does not necessarily understand how the hospital itself can impact on coping. Neither are developmental factors recognised which may affect changes in individual coping styles, and the effect this, combined with social changes such as changing staff and external, home-related events, may have on both child and family in their efforts to cope with environmental stressors and long-term health problems.

Power relationships in a medical model are, in my experience, rarely considered in a real-time context – especially when working with disempowered children i.e. disempowered through both their 'lack of voice' in a hospital environment where they are dependent on adult care, and also through their lack of developmental maturity, in comparison to adults. As one of the professional caregivers responsible in supporting these children's psychosocial needs, I need to be particularly careful in analysing my interventions offered through play therapy and any subsequent advocacy of the child's needs when working in a multi-disciplinary setting.

This study has offered me the opportunity to reflect on such issues and consider the insights I have gained through this analysis – of whether I have met the intended aims for the study and what I actually implemented.

Causal network

In attempting to relate the variables of my study I have analysed correspondences, discrepancies and ambivalences through four key areas:

1. Hospital admission and coping
2. Play therapy intervention and coping
3. Hospital admission and social impact
4. Play therapy intervention and social impact.

Hospital admission and coping

My findings would suggest that the impact of the hospital environment is not being recognised by hospital staff when considering this child's stress reactions and coping abilities e.g. the mother was the only adult to identify that her child is affected by a poorly structured or unpredictable environment. . . . There is an expectation that the child will be able to verbalise her needs and feelings – and that stress effects caused by the hospital environment itself will not be actively taken into account when considering her ability to do so.

Play therapy intervention and coping

My findings would suggest that the stories arising out of the play therapy sessions have a high correlation of agreement between the adults' and child's views regarding the likelihood of hospital links being expressed through these metaphoric themes . . .

Hospital admission and social impact

There is a particular discrepancy in how the consultant rates the child regarding her relationships, when compared to other adults. Bearing in mind that his was the only male response throughout the study, I suggest additional variables, which may be affecting this result:

- The child's absent father may provide the potential for conflicts being projected onto this consultant
- There is a discourse around gender and power relationships, which would seem to relate to medical concepts of the patient/doctor relationship, which expects the adult to provide guidance to the young who are in turn expected to accept such guidance.

Play therapy intervention and social impact

My findings would suggest insights are to be found in the child's stories, but that there is some weakness in my design, particularly in evaluating this area.

. . .

My omissions have made me relook at how decisions are made which include or exclude children from such a research process – and potentially from the decisions affecting their lives. To avoid this in the future it would perhaps be better to design all questionnaires using a child-centred perspective.

Summary

I can conclude that the findings I have analysed allow insights into the co-constructed relationship between the adult therapist and the child. . . . It has enabled both the child and myself to explore the concepts of coping as I have intended, identifying 'camouflaged' aspects of stress, the hermeneutic orientation widening my perspectives on the impact of hospitalisation and how school-aged children's needs are possibly being misunderstood regarding coping styles . . .

Play therapy intervention would seem to offer potential as an alternative construction to help understand children's coping with hospitalisation, taking into account their developmental changes when seeking to identify the vulnerabilities they may have. It also offers a familiar, child-centred medium regarding play, which is not solely reliant on the child's verbalisation of needs. There is also the possibility to use metaphor and symbol to help a child negotiate and explore identities and power relations between self and others. In doing so I find it essential that the child's behaviour is looked at not only with adult's eyes, but also from the child's own stance, taking seriously what they tell us about how they think they cope with life both in the context of hospital, but also in the linked areas of home and school. Play therapy can allow the child to use a safe environment, where metaphor can distance the child enough from the pressures they may feel in the direct verbalisation of feelings – but encourages them to explore these through their use of play resources. It is here that we may build some of the bridges necessary in order to understand their evolving needs.

Hermeneutic research

An exciting method of research is to present a play therapy intervention with a client or group as a hermeneutic activity shaped by an interest in the evolving narrative. Hermeneutics in this context could be described as the analysis of texts presented by clients during a therapy session to explore aspects of the intervention. This kind of research is an aspect of new paradigm research, which is qualitative and explores particular truths within a social interaction.

Hermeneutics is defined as the art or science of the interpretation of texts. The meaning of the text depends on the interplay between the storyteller's narrative and the interpreter's construction, that is on the interpersonal context in which meaning is constructed.

Ricoeur (1981) defines hermeneutics as the theory of the operations of understanding in their relation to the interpretation of texts. He states that

the meaning of text lies not behind the text but in front of it. The meaning is not something hidden but something disclosed. What gives rise to understanding is that which points towards a possible world, by means of the non-ostensive references of the text. Texts speak of possible worlds and of possible ways of orientating oneself in these worlds.

(p. 177)

The language of hermeneutics explores the human subject as one who comes to realise that he can only interpret himself by interpreting the 'signs' of an external world not his own. He is an embodied being who discovers that he is placed in language before he possesses himself in consciousness.

Le Vay (1998) explores these themes in relation to play therapy. He states that the reflexive quality within the interpretative process leads us to the notion of Ricoeur's hermeneutic circle, which can be viewed as a metaphor for describing the contextual nature of knowledge and experience. The hermeneutic circle describes the continuous movement back and forth between the part and the whole.

> It is in this sense that I believe that a model of *narrative identity* can facilitate a process in play therapy through which the notions of narrative on a local level, and identity on a global level can be brought together in a circular, dialectic process of understanding in which a child's narrative expressive state can provide clues as to how they make sense and order themselves and their experiences in relation to the wider personal and social world that they are part of. Identity is revealed through discourse and it is the analysis and interpretation of this discourse, in the form of text, which provides the insight into the narrative identity of the child at that particular moment in time.

(p. 15)

The social construction of identity

As a play therapist I use social construction theories to underpin the methods and structures in helping children make sense of difficult experiences. In fact I define play therapy itself as a social construction with rules and boundaries devised and agreed by child and therapist.

When we begin to research the meanings of the texts in play therapy interventions we are able to integrate the hermeneutic approach to the analysis of meaning of particular texts within the social construction frame we use as play therapists.

In order to consider the analysis of texts in a hermeneutic study we need to recap on social construction theory, which describes the construction of identity through narratives of the self.

Burr (1995) states that social construction theory suggests that all ways of understanding are historically and culturally relative, specific to particular cultures and periods of history, products of that culture and history dependent on particular social and economic arrangements prevailing in that culture at that time.

Knowledge is sustained by social processes. Our knowledge of the world is constructed between people. Shared versions of knowledge are constructed in the course of everyday lives together. We make use of words in conversations to perform actions in a moral universe.

Much of the sorting of stories and narratives in play therapy is about actions in a moral universe. The 'goodies' and the 'baddies', what is a monster and are all monsters bad? We play around with versions of understanding until we find a satisfactory meaning together which encompasses the consequences in our particular culture and time.

Paul, aged 8, told this story:

> There was once a horrible monster.
> His name was Skeleton.
> He had no body, just a face and everything.
> He was sad and lonely.
> One day he met another monster called Joe.
> They liked each other and became friends.
> The way they were with each other was to be kind and not hit each other.

I said that I was puzzled that they were called monsters. What had they done to deserve that title? Paul said that:

> People liked them even though they were monsters.
> They didn't have mums and dads. They were born without them.

I asked how they managed that. Paul said:

> They come from outer space in America.
> So they didn't know who their parents were
> And this made them sad.

We began a discussion about the meaning of monsters and the meaning of superheroes. Paul was sad and ashamed that he did not live with his parents and to him they seemed lost in outer space. To have no parents was a humiliation and must mean that you are 'bad' so therefore a 'monster' – even though you are kind and people liked you.

These conversations are important to children to define who they are and sort out some of their confusions about their world. It is the role of the therapist to help them sort out confusion and work through the cognitive distortions which children might have about their family and themselves. If we simply reflect back what children are saying then it is difficult for them to reach a satisfactory understanding of their situation. Of course the therapist does not 'tell' them her or his understanding but through questions, talk about meaning, the child and therapist negotiate together.

Malone (1997) states that each person's life is lived as a series of conversations. It is in the flowing reciprocal exchange of conversation that the self becomes real. Without such talk the self would be inconceivable because it would lack the symbolic medium necessary for self-presentation. Paul is sorting ideas about his origins, being friends, being awful, being a monster, but also being kind. These are moral dilemmas and need to be heard. In the therapeutic space and through the relationship with the therapist he can define himself and present himself.

Goffman (1959) states that the self is immanently social, an interactional achievement, a performed character, a dramatic effect, and we craft our behaviour so that it makes sense to others. In this frame conversations and selves are both interactional accomplishments requiring trust, dependency and co-ordination. The presentation of self in a social event is the principal way for others to know who we are.

Lax (1992) states that in therapy the interaction itself is where the text exists and where new narratives of life emerge. This unfolding text happens between people. Clients unfold the story of their lives in conjunction with a specific therapist therefore the therapist is always co-author of the story. So the resulting text is neither the client's nor the therapist's story but a co-construction of the two.

Play therapy is a social event with its own social rules and processes. It is also an interaction, which is semiotic because it should be understood as an assemblage of signs. All talk must be self-referential so child and therapist interpret utterances as signs, which stand for a larger self. The child makes assumptions about the life of the therapist from their own self-references so Paul considers me as superhero or monster and himself as monster as these are his categories of people at this time.

This social construction frame of intervention can be researched through a hermeneutic analysis of some of the texts presented by child and therapist in their meetings with each other.

The interpretation of texts

In play therapy children tell stories as containers of their experiences. The therapist listens to the child's stories in an equal relationship and together they share the drama of the story as the meaning unfolds.

In *Storied Lives*, Rosenwald and Ochberg (1992) define four themes in the way people tell stories about their lives. First, the stories people tell about themselves are interesting not only for the events and characters they describe but in the construction of the stories themselves. What people tell and what they leave out, whether they speak of themselves as heroes or victims, all say something about the way they construct their identities. Second, the identity forming nature of personal stories may be constrained or stunted and this inability to tell their stories can affect their lives. Third, it is assumed that all stories are told and that all self-knowledge is understood within the narrative frames each culture provides for its members. For example a child may fear to tell a story because she has been told that it is 'rude'. Fourth, it is possible to enlarge the range of personal narratives. So perhaps a child can explore a story about a hero who is not a victim and extend their range of roles to incorporate into their range of personal stories.

A hermeneutic analysis in play therapy is a way to explore themes presented in the stories and play of children or aspects of the interactions between child and therapist through a textual analysis of the communication.

Validity

The validity of the interpretation of texts is an important aspect of new paradigm research. Packer and Addison (1994) describe four approaches to validate an interpretative account. First, *coherence* in that the interpretation should make sense. A good interpretative account will scrutinise and check an interpretation that appears coherent by searching out and focusing on material that doesn't make sense. Second, *external evidence* which means seeking out evidence that exists outside of the account to test the interpretations. This includes the intention of the participant and what the text means to them in the present. Third, *consensus*; the seeking of a consensus among other researchers. A good interpretation should be able to be proposed to others and to make sense to them. It would also need to acknowledge the possibility of other interpretations. Fourth, *practical implications*; that there should be an examining of the relationship between the interpretation and what implications it has for future events.

This deepening of the textual understanding by incorporating the ideas of the client and other connected individuals is called the hermeneutic circle. The intention is not to end the analysis with a definitive interpretation but a circle of interpretations, which hold together the complexity of the text. Within the exchange of understanding there must be some degree of consensus among researchers while incorporating a diversity of meanings.

A hermeneutic research project

Liz Hiles works as a freelance play therapist for social services departments and health authorities in the South East of England. She works with a wide variety of client groups and with the children's extended families and carers as well as individuals in the systems within which they are living. The therapist wanted to look at the repetition of stories from children in play therapy. She describes how she set up her project.

Extract from setting up the research project

In my work as a freelance play therapist I see many children who have suffered trauma. In play therapy children use materials to create stories whereby they explore issues and feelings at a safe distance using symbol and metaphor. The use of stories is therefore of great interest to me in my work.

Many children use repetition in the way they play and I became particularly interested in the use of repetition in story making.

For the purpose of my research it was important to focus my thinking and reading around one particular mode of enquiry.

I therefore decided to focus on one particular child who frequently creates stories and narratives in our work together. I became interested in his use of repetitive story themes and in the reasons why he re-creates these stories. I question what purpose it serves for him. This interest formed the basis of my research project.

My own belief is that the recreation of the story themes helps this child to gain a better understanding of his life experiences, which in turn helps him to gain mastery over these experiences.

My research hypothesis became: Do repetitive story themes help a child in play therapy gain mastery over difficult experiences?

The therapist worked with an 8-year-old boy called Simon on her project. She gained the appropriate ethical permissions and permission from Simon to use his stories. He also agreed to talk about his stories as part of the project. Simon had been in care for some time. He had recently learned that his father had not died in a car accident as he had been told, but had committed suicide by jumping in front of a train. It was thought that Simon had been sexually abused by his father.

The therapist selected two stories by Simon, which were repeated and referenced by him during play therapy. She describes the stories and the analysis of the texts.

The following extracts are taken from the research.

A selection of the texts

For the purpose of this research I will be focusing on the repetitive use of two stories. Simon told the first story in his fifth play therapy session and this was the session following Simon's knowledge of his father's suicide. Simon started this particular session playing with the slime and talking about what he had been doing that week in school. He went on to explore the toys and select some for play. He then said that he would like to make up a story and we agreed that I would write his story down with others he had created in previous sessions.

Simon selected a Playmobil figure to which he gave his own name. He chose a toy motorbike, and a large car in which he put another figure representing a driver. Simon also chose to use some slime and Buzz Lightyear. Simon enacted his story with the figures and narrated it as he went along. This was his story:

> *The adventure*
> One day there was a little boy; eight years old called Simon.
> He bought himself a BMW motorbike. It was red.
> One day he was riding along.
> He suddenly stopped because there was a green mess on the road.
> He ran back to tell the others.
> One person didn't listen – the car.
> He was driving along and the green mess leaked out on to his car window.
> The car went all over the place.
> The little boy Simon went down the road where the green mess was.
> He ran to the car and got off his bike.
> Buzz Lightyear heard everything and flew down and asked the boy Simon what had happened.
> He grabbed the clay off the car and chucked it at the boy because he had chucked the clay at the car
> And he was sucked up into the green mess and couldn't get it off.
> From that day onwards he would never do something like that again.
> The End.

Following this story, Simon drew a picture of the man in the car and the slime.

We talked about some of the feelings that the people may have felt, i.e. the boy and the man in the car, as well as the reasons Buzz Lightyear came along.

Eight weeks later Simon told the story again. This time it has a different title.

> *The boy in the street*
> One day there was a boy on a BMX motorbike.
> His name was Simon.

One day he saw a pink thing in the road.
He stopped.
He turned back to tell the others in the city.
There was one person that didn't listen – the man in the car.
He drove where the pink stuff was.
He drove into it by accident.
A man who was a Ninja jumped down and got the pink stuff off the car.
The boy on the BMX motorbike came along.
He chucked it at the boy because the boy had chucked it at the car.
From that day onwards he wouldn't do anything like that again in his life.
The End.

Following the story, we talked about the similarities between this story and the one he had created in a previous session. Simon said that this was his favourite story.

Extracts from the therapist's analysis of the stories

The thing that struck me first about Simon's use of these particular stories is that he used his own name and age in them. This therefore leads me to believe that he is identifying himself in these stories and therefore not distancing himself as he might have chosen to do and has done in other stories.

I think the car may resemble Simon's father's car, which he had believed for so long had been involved in an accident, which had killed his father. It may also have resembled the train, which did kill his father, leaving a 'mess' in front of it, as in the story the green stuff leaked out on to his car window. The car went all over the place, i.e. a collision.

I believe that the stories are about the death by suicide of his father and the confusion Simon feels about this. I also feel that there may be some feelings of disgust regarding the possible sexual abuse of Simon by his father in the mess he talks about, as well as the actual physical mess of his father's remains following suicide.

I believe that the boy Simon in the story desperately wanted to be heard and do something to stop the potential disaster just as Simon feels now when he reflects on his father's death . . .

I wonder if Simon was expressing how it feels not to be heard when in the story he says that the man did not listen. Perhaps he feels that his father did not hear him regarding the abuse or the fact that Simon feels sad or maybe angry that his father is no longer alive to hear him and what he has to say. It would seem likely that Simon has some ambivalence regarding his relationship with his father. This is a very common theme for many children who have suffered abuse, when although they feel angry with the perpetrator for what was done, they still love them.

The superhero seems to be a magical theme of someone who could come and save the day, but Simon was able to make a link with reality that it was too late and nothing could be done and he felt helpless.

Perhaps the mess described in 'he was sucked up into the green mess and couldn't get it off' expresses what it is like to be enveloped in a mess of confusion and many mixed emotions i.e. grief, anger, fear, abandonment, hopelessness, helplessness with many unanswered questions and many things left unsaid. This is then an all-encompassing feeling perhaps even of suffocation – not being able to get it off – having to live through this time and make sense of it.

The therapist then describes what Simon thought about his own stories.

Extracts from Simon's reflections on his stories

Simon said that these two stories were his favourites because of the slime in them. He said that he said his own name in them because the name is famous as it is his.

I asked Simon about the repetition of his stories and why he had repeated them. Simon said that it was because he could not think of a different story or title. He said that the reason for this was because 'sometimes I just can't think about it because it is too difficult.'

Simon recognised that many of his stories have the same title like *The Boy in the Street*. He said the street is a familiar place to him because he goes to the street a lot with his foster carers . . .

Simon's reflections are then explored by the therapist to widen the level of understanding about the stories.

Extracts from therapist's reflections on Simon's analysis of his stories

> Simon commented that repetition of his stories gets rid of all his sad memories. He said that by talking about his dad it gets rid of his bad feelings. When I asked him for an example of what he meant, Simon said, 'about my dad dying on purpose.' This was the first time Simon had acknowledged that his stories were about his father. Simon said that by making up these stories, it makes him feel a lot better.
>
> Simon said that slime was horrible, like rubbish and glue mixed together. I wonder if this is about disgust or just the mess and confusion he feels about his past, or whether it has something to do with the remains of his father.

As part of the hermeneutic circle the therapist has examined the texts, asked the author for his comments, then analysed her view of the author's view. This means that validation has been tested through the coherence of the interpretation and the external evidence by the description of the intention of the client. The therapist then sought consensus by asking other researchers to comment on the texts. This was done through a questionnaire about the two texts. The therapist selected a play therapist and a teacher to be researchers for the project.

The play therapist's view of the stories

This was a response to a questionnaire about the two stories. The therapist also had a copy of the stories and a brief life history of Simon.

The play therapist named the main themes in the two stories as being guilt, responsibility, death, warning/alerting and confusion.

She thought that the 'mess' in the story might resemble danger, the confusion of Simon's family life, a sense of leaky muddles or a cause of death, and also possibly something to do with sexual abuse.

She thought that the car was a metaphor for his dad and that the superhero might resemble a mixture of retribution/punishment and rescue.

The reasons for Simon repeating this story in his play therapy sessions might be to create meaningful images to help him in his attempts to make sense of his world and help him make sense of the sequence of events and to explore his perceptions of his role within his family life and the death of his dad.

The teacher's analysis of the stories

This was a response to a questionnaire about the two stories. The teacher also had a copy of the stories and a brief life history of Simon

She thought that the themes were vehicles, a boy who came across a mess/accident, a hero figure who takes control but doesn't allow the boy to escape, the person who did not listen and therefore was in trouble and she thought that the last sentence of both stories was expressing the thought of trying to look ahead but also still remembering the past and possibly feeling guilty about a past event.

She thought that the mess might resemble what Simon imagines his father would have looked like after death. She also commented that 'mess' is a word used by adults when discussing problems/outcomes of difficulties.

She thought that the car might represent the vehicle such as the train or in place of the car Simon had thought for so long had been the cause of his father's death. Either way she felt that it was a life threatening force/thing, which ran out of control despite being warned. She felt it was linked to the death of his father.

She thought that the superhero might be Simon's conscience, an angel/god/power/a magical figure or a respected adult helping him deal with problems.

She thought that the reason why Simon frequently repeated this story in play therapy was because the events cannot be forgotten; by repeating and so continuing to remember, Simon hopes to make sense of the senseless. She thought that Simon might hope to resolve the mess in some way and he is mourning the death and wonders how guilty he is himself of involvement leading up to it. He may also want someone else to take charge of his feelings but still needs some punishment – i.e. the mess sticking to him and he could not get it off. He may also be hopeful that in the future things will get better and the bad things might go away and he will have learned from it. This links with the last line of the stories 'he wouldn't do anything like that again in his life.'

These interpretations led to a deepening of understanding about the texts, which added to an understanding of Simon's use of stories in play therapy. The therapist then examined the other stories used by Simon. 'The analysis of repetition of themes in other texts was demonstrated by charts and tables and this showed his continued use of cars, superheroes and slime in eighteen of his stories presented in play therapy.'

Extract from final evaluation

The final evaluation demonstrated that the repetition of the stories helped Simon in four aspects of his lived experiences.

> There is a consensus that repetition did help Simon. Congruent with all those questioned are the following processes: the trauma of his father's suicide, the repair of his sense of self through the narrative process, coping with his new physical environment, the use of repetition to cope with post-traumatic stress.

In his last meeting with the therapist Simon said that he had benefited from the therapy and had one last story.

The man in the street
One day there was a man called Simon.
If you read Simon chapter one then you would know that Simon chucked clay at the man in the car.
Simon was now an ambulance driver and the man wanted to get his revenge back.
He chucked some clay in the road.
Simon wasn't stupid.
He saw Joshua chuck it in the road and quickly turned the steering wheel on the ambulance.
The man Joshua was a murderer.
He opened the ambulance doors and jumped in.
Simon turned a sharp corner and made Joshua fly back in to the ambulance door.
Simon had to get the fire extinguisher and spray it all over Joshua.
He broke one of the doors and was slipping out.
His feet were scraping on the floor.
Suddenly he fell out and landed on the gunge.
The ambulance stopped and Simon got out.

He took Joshua to the police station and he was arrested.
Simon came to visit him.
And from that day onwards Joshua would never do anything
like that again.
The End.'

Conclusions

New ideas for research are exciting developments and help in
defining and shaping therapeutic interventions to evaluate what
works for the client and to refine what is helpful in the social
context of the life of children who have experienced distressing life
events. It is vital that the therapist is able to evaluate practice for
the safety and protection of clients and the development of new
ways to support the needs of children.

The work of play therapists is often derided as 'easy, just playing
with children, anybody can do that' so to research what happens
between the child and therapist and to think about what the child
says when engrossed in imaginative play shared with a responsive
adult is important as a way to value children and their play and to
value the work and training of the therapist who supports and
respects the child.

References

Aries, P. (1960 (1986)) *Centuries of Childhood*. Harmondsworth: Penguin.

Axline, V. (1969) *Play Therapy*. New York: Ballantine Books.

Bateson, G. (1972) *Steps to an Ecology of Mind*. New York: Chandler.

Bateson, G. (1995) 'A theory of play and fantasy', *Psychiatric Research Reports* 2: 39–51.

Baudrillard, J. (1993) *The Transparency of Evil* (trans. J. Benedict). London: Verso.

Belsky, J., Nezworski, J. and Lawrence, T. (1988) 'Child-Adult Relationship Experimental Index (CARE Index)'. In *The Clinical Implications of Attachment*. New Jersey: Erlbaum Associates.

Borges, J. (1967) *The Book of Imaginary Beings*. Harmondsworth: Penguin.

Bowlby, J. (1969) *Attachment and Loss (vol. 1)*. Harmondsworth: Penguin.

Bowlby, J. (1971) *Attachment and Loss (vol. 2)*. Harmondsworth: Pelican Books.

Bowlby, J. (1973) *Attachment and Loss (vol. 3)*. Harmondsworth: Pelican Books.

Boyd, A. (1999) *Life's Little Deconstruction Book*. London: Penguin Books Ltd.

Breggin, P. (1998) *Talking Back to Ritalin: What Doctors Aren't Telling You About Stimulants for Children*. Monroe: Common Courage Press.

Bronfenbrenner, U. (1979) *The Ecology of Human Development*. Cambridge, MA: Harvard University Press.

Burr, V. (1995) *An Introduction to Social Constructionism*. London: Routledge.

Carle, E. (1995) *Draw Me a Star*. London: Picture Puffin.

Carroll, J. (2001) *Highlight No. 180 Play Therapy*. London: National Children's Bureau.

Cattanach, A. (1992) *Play Therapy with Abused Children*. London: Jessica Kingsley Publishers.

Cattanach, A. (1994) *Play Therapy Where the Sky Meets the Underworld*. London: Jessica Kingsley Publishers.

Cattanach, A. (1997) *Children's Stories in Play Therapy*. London: Jessica Kingsley Publishers.

Cattanach, A. (1999) 'Co-construction in play therapy'. In A. Cattanach (ed.), *Process in the Arts Therapies*. London: Jessica Kingsley Publishers.

Child, N. (1996) 'How true story telling lost its place', *Context* 28: 34–37.

Coppock, V. (2002) 'Medicalising children's behaviour'. In B. Franklin (ed.), *The New Handbook of Children's Rights*. London: Routledge.

Department of Health 12 Key Points on Consent: The Law in England. Ref: 23618 1p 25ok Mar 01 (COL).

Department of Health (2001) Establishing the New Health Professions Council. Department of Health Publications, PO Box 777, London SE1 6XH. Ref 23624.

De Mause, L. (ed.) (1976) *The History of Childhood*. London: Souvenir Press.

Dighton, R. (2001) 'Toward a definition of play therapy', *Play Therapy* Issue 28, p. 910.

Dunbar, J. and Gliori, D. (1998) *Tell Me Something Happy Before I Go to Sleep*. London: Corgi Books.

Dunn, J. (1987) 'Understanding feelings: the early stages'. In J. Bruner and H. Haste (eds), *Making Sense*. London: Methuen & Co. Ltd.

Dunn, J. (1993) *Young Children's Close Relationships*. London: Sage.

Foucault, M. (1984) 'Introduction'. In P. Rabinow (ed.), *The Foucault Reader*. London: Penguin Books.

Gittins, D. (1998) *The Child In Question*. Basingstoke: Macmillan Press Ltd.

Goffman, E. (1959) *The Presentation of Self in Everyday Life*. New York: Doubleday.

Goldson, B. (1997) 'Childhood: an introduction to historical and theoretical analysis'. In P. Scraton (ed.), *'Childhood' in 'Crisis'?* London: UCL Press.

Grainger, R. (1990) *Drama and Healing. The Roots of Dramatherapy*. London: Jessica Kingsley Publishers.

Greig, A. and Taylor, J. (1999) *Doing Research with Children*. London: Sage.

Hallidan, G. (1991) 'The child as project and the child as being: parents' ideas as frames of reference', *Children and Society* 5(4): 334–346.

Hanawalt, B. (1993) *Growing Up in Mediaeval London*. Oxford: Oxford University Press.

Haring, K. (1994) *Nina's Book of Little Things*. New York: Prestel-Verlay.

Hart, A. and Thomas, H. (2000) 'Controversial attachments. The indirect treatment of fostered and adopted children via parent co-therapy', *Attachment and Human Behaviour* 2(3): 306–327.

Hendrick, H. (1990) 'Constructions and reconstructions of British childhood'. In A. James and A. Prout (eds), *Constructing and Reconstructing Childhood*. London: Falmer.

Hopkins, G.M. (1982) 'As kingfishers catch fire, dragonflies draw flame'. In S. Heaney and T. Hughes (eds), *The Rattle Bag*. London: Faber & Faber.

Human Rights Watch *Easy Targets 2001* On the internet: http// www.hrw.org/children

Ideus, K. and Cooper, P. (eds) (1995) *ADHD: Educational, Medical and Cultural Issues*. Kent: Association of Workers for Children with Emotional and Behavioural Difficulties.

James, A. and Prout, A. (eds) (1990) *Constructing and Reconstructing Childhood: Comtemporary Issues in the Sociological Study of Childhood*. London: Falmer.

Jamieson, L. and Toynbee, C. (1992) *Country Bairns*. Edinburgh: Edinburgh University Press.

Janesick, V. (1994) 'The dance of qualitative research design: metaphor, methodology and meaning'. In N. Denzin and Y. Lincoln (eds), *Handbook of Qualitative Research*. London: Sage.

Jenks, C. (1996) *Childhood*. London: Routledge.

Jennings, S. (1990) *Dramatherapy with Families, Groups and Individuals*. London: Routledge & Kegan Paul.

Jennings, S. (1998) *Introduction to Dramatherapy*. London: Jessica Kingsley Publishers.

Jensen, P., Mrazek, D., Knapp, P. et al. (1997) 'Evolution and revolution in child psychiatry: ADHD as a disorder of adaption', *Journal of the American Academy of Child and Adolescent Psychiatry* 36(12): 1672–1681.

Johnson, J., Christie, J. and Yawkey, T. (1987) *Play and Early Childhood Development*. USA: Harper Collins.

Kaduson, H. (1997) 'Play therapy for children with ADHD'. In H. Kaduson, D. Cangelosi and C. Schaefer (eds), *The Playing Cure*. New Jersey: Jason Aronson Inc.

Knell, S. (1995) *Cognitive–Behavioural Play Therapy*. New Jersey: Jason Aronson Inc.

Lax, W. (1992) 'Post-modern thinking in a clinical practice'. In K. Gergen and S. Mcnamee (eds), *Therapy as Social Construction*. London: Sage.

Lax, W. (1999) *Definitions of Narrative Therapy*. Dulwich Centre Conference on Narrative: Adelaide.

Le Vay, D. (1998) *The Self is a Telling*. Unpublished thesis, University of Surrey, Roehampton.

Le Vay, D. (2002) 'The self is a telling'. In A. Cattanach (ed.), *The Story So Far. Play Therapy Narratives*. London: Jessica Kingsley Publishers.

Malone, M. (1997) *Worlds of Talk*. Cambridge: Polity Press.

McMillan, D. (ed.) (2000) *The Scotswoman at Home and Abroad*. Glasgow: Public Association for Scottish Literary Studies.

Marschak, M., Jernburg, A. and Booth, P. (1993) *Theraplay, Helping Parents and Children Build Better Relationships Through Attachment-based Play*. San Francisco: Jossey-Bass.

Meldrum, B. (1996) Unpublished lectures on Play Therapy. London: University of Surrey, Roehampton.

Meldrum, B. (1998) Unpublished lectures on Research. London: University of Surrey, Roehampton.

Mental Health Foundation (1998) *The Big Picture: Promoting Children and Young People's Mental Health*. London: Mental Health Foundation.

O'Connor, K. (1983) 'The Color-Your-Life Technique'. In C. Schaefer and K. O'Connor (eds), *Handbook of Play Therapy*. Chichester: John Wiley & Sons.

O'Connor, K. (1999) 'Child protector, confidant: structured group ecosystem play therapy'. In D. Sweeney and L. Homeyer (eds), *The Handbook of Group Play Therapy*. San Francisco: Jossey-Bass.

Opie, I. (1992) 'Introduction'. In I. Opie and P. Opie (eds), *I Saw Esau*. London: Walker Books.

Packer, M. and Addison, R. (1994) 'Evaluating an interpretative account'. In M. Packer and R. Addison (eds), *Entering the Circle: Hermeneutic Investigations in Psychology*. Albany: State University of New York Press.

Pellegrini, D. and Smith, P. (1998) 'An overview of the functions of play', *Child Psychology and Psychiatry* 3(2): 51–57.

Piaget, J. (1977) *The Language and Thought of the Child*. London: Routledge & Kegan Paul.

Pollock, L. (1983) *Forgotten Children*. Cambridge: Cambridge University Press.

Prout, A. and James, A. (1990) 'A new paradigm for the sociology of childhood'. In A. James and A. Prout (eds), *Constructing and Reconstructing Childhood*. Basingstoke: The Falmer Press.

Richardson, A. (2001) 'Getting set for regulation in healthcare', *Healthcare Counselling and Psychotherapy Journal* 1(2): 5–7.

Ricoeur, P. (1981) *Hermeneutics and the Human Sciences*. Cambridge: Cambridge University Press.

Riddell, M. (2001) '*What are Children For?*' *Observer* 9 September.

Robinson, B. (1997 'Draw-a-person inquiry'. In *Psychotherapy of Abused and Neglected Children*. London: Guilford Press.

Robson, C. (1993) *Real World Research*. Oxford: Blackwell.

Rosenwald, G. and Ochberg, R. (1992) *Storied Lives: the Cultural Politics of Self-Understanding.* Yale: Yale University Press.

Ryan, V. and Wilson, K. (1996) *Case Studies in Non-directive Play Therapy.* London: Ballière Tindall.

Save the Children, Scotland (2002). On the internet: www.childrenunbeatable.org.uk

Scott Nash, M. (2002) 'The Wounded Hero'. In A. Cattanach (ed.), *The Story So Far. Play Therapy Narratives.* London: Jessica Kingsley Publishers.

Smith, B. (1991) *A Child's Guide to Bad Behaviour.* London: Pavilion Books.

Stake, R. (1995) *The Art of Case Study Research.* London: Sage.

Sutton-Smith, B. (1994) 'Does play prepare the future?' In J. Goldstein (ed.), *Toys, Play and Child Development.* Cambridge: Cambridge University Press.

Vandenberg, B. (1986) 'Play, myth and hope'. In R. van der Kooij and J. Hellendoorn (eds), *Play, Play Therapy, Play Research.* Lisse: Swets and Zerlinger BV.

Van Fleet, R. (2000) 'Short-term play therapy for families with chronic illness'. In H. Kaduson and C. Schaefer (eds), *Short-Term Play Therapy for Children.* New York: The Guilford Press.

Vygotsky, L. (1978) *Mind in Society. The Development of Higher Psychological Processes.* Cambridge, MA: Harvard University Press.

Walsh, J. (1999) *What If?* London: Jonathan Cape.

Warner, M. (1994) *Managing Monsters.* London: Vintage UK.

Watson, R. (2002) 'All that Glitters is not Gold. The Adoption Process as a Rise of Passage'. In A. Cattanach (ed.), *The Story So Far. Play Therapy Narratives.* London: Jessica Kingsley Publishers.

West, J. (1992 (1996)) *Child Centred Play Therapy.* London: Arnold.

Wilson, K., Kendrick, P. and Ryan, V. (1992) *Play Therapy. A Non-directive Approach for Children and Adolescents.* London: Ballière Tindall.

Winnicott, D. (1974) *Playing and Reality.* London: Tavistock.

Index